A Student's Manual
of New Testament
Greek Accents

A Student's Manual of New Testament Greek Accents

D. A. Carson

BAKER BOOK HOUSE
Grand Rapids, Michigan 49506

ISBN: 0-8010-2494-3

Printed in the United States of America

Many of the sentences in the exercises of this *Manual* have been taken from J. W. Wenham, *The Elements of New Testament Greek*, copyrighted in 1965 by the Dean and Chapter of Ely and published by Cambridge University Press, and are reproduced (sometimes in adapted form) by permission.

To my students past and present
whose wholesome curiosity does not permit them
to remain in ignorance about any of the ink marks
on the pages of the Greek New Testament,
this book is affectionately dedicated.

Contents

Preface   9

1. Background and Preliminary Definitions   13

2. The General Rules of Accent   19

3. The Basic Rule for Verbs   22

4. Contract Verbs   24

5. The Basic Rule for Nouns; Nouns of the First and Second
   Declensions   27

6. Second Declension Neuter Nouns; First Declension Feminine Nouns;
   The Definite Article   32

7. First Declension Masculine Nouns; Indeclinable Words   39

8. Second and First Declension Adjectives   43

9. Enclitics and Proclitics   47

10. The Imperfect Indicative Active; Compound Verbs   53

11. Demonstratives; αὐτός, ἑαυτόν, and ἀλλήλους; Imperfect of εἰμί   56

12. More Indeclinable Words; Present and Imperfect Indicative
    Passive   60

13. The Relative Pronoun; The Present Imperative; More Indeclinable
    Words   63

14. First and Second Person Personal Pronouns, Possessive Adjectives,
    and Reflexive Pronouns; More Indeclinable Words   67

15. The Present Infinitive; δύναμαι; The Future Active   70

16. The Verbal Stem; The Middle Voice; The Future of εἰμί   73

17. The First Aorist Active; The Second Aorist Active   75

18. Liquid Verbs; More Indeclinable Words   80

19. First and Second Aorist Middle   83

20. Third Declension Masculine and Feminine Nouns with Consonant Stems   85

21. Third Declension Neuter Nouns   90

22. Third Declension Adjectives; Interrogative and Indefinite Pronouns   93

23. Third Declension Nouns with Vowel Stems   98

24. Adjectives and Pronouns of the Third and First Declensions; Numerals   102

25. Comparison of Adjectives; Adverbs   108

26. Perfect and Pluperfect   111

27. Aorist and Future Passives   113

28. Participles; More Adverbs   115

29. The Subjunctive Mood   122

30. The Optative Mood   125

31. More on Contract Verbs; Verbs in -αω and -οω   127

32. The -μι Verbs: τίθημι   131

33. The -μι Verbs: δίδωμι   134

34. The -μι Verbs: ἵστημι   136

35. Other -μι Verbs   139

36. Some New Testament Passages   141

37. The Next Steps   143

Some Accented Principal Parts   146

Summary of Accent Rules   149

Key to the Exercises   154

Preface

In many institutions in the English-speaking world, Greek, whether Attic or Hellenistic, is now being taught without accents. For those studying New Testament Greek, this pedagogical approach has been made especially common by the wide circulation of the book by J. W. Wenham, *The Elements of New Testament Greek*, first published by Cambridge University Press in 1965. The advantages are obvious, especially for those whose goal is to gain a working knowledge of the New Testament for pastoral purposes, but who have no intention of gaining real expertise in the language. The early stages of learning the language seem to present so much new and challenging material that to eliminate the need to learn accents is to prompt vast relief.

Not all instructors of the Greek language have been convinced that this is the best way to teach the language; but I do not want to debate the point in theoretical terms. My experience so far, however, suggests that the best students, those who are able to go fastest or farthest, benefit from learning proper accentuation at the earliest stages. To do so removes ignorance about another set of strange black marks on the printed page, and therefore eliminates a *psychological* barrier.

Be that as it may, I suspect that more than half the students who study beginning Greek, especially New Testament Greek, are not taught the rudiments of accentuation—even when the text used is not Wenham's *Elements*. At least Wenham warns his readers what he is omitting!

My own pilgrimage as a student of Greek is not reassuring. I first studied classical Greek; but at the North American university where I did my work, accents were not taught. Subsequently I studied at a seminary, preparing for pastoral ministry; and again I was reassured that I didn't need to know anything about accents at that stage. Out of sheer curiosity I tried to pick up some of the rudiments myself; but these were quickly forgotten in the busy rounds of parish ministry.

Some years later, I went on for doctoral studies in the New Testament. When I submitted my dissertation at Cambridge University, I had sorted out most of the accents; but I was profoundly grateful for Dr. Colin Hemer, who graciously checked my typescript, and eliminated the rest of the errors—including a would-be polysyllabic enclitic. Mortified, I resolved to learn principles of accentuation so well I would never be caught short again.

Immediately I confronted a new difficulty. The introductory grammars which deal with accents scatter their information throughout their pages; and some of that information I soon discovered to be correct for Attic Greek, but incorrect for the Greek of the New Testament. The little book (49 pp.) by A. J. Koster, *A Practical Guide for the Writing of the Greek Accents* (Leiden: Brill, 1962) deals only with Classical Greek, and is in any case rather terse, and not without a healthy share of misprints. The large grammars dealing with Hellenistic Greek make no allowance for their readers' ignorance, presupposing, for instance, an ability to distinguish between a proparoxytone and a properispomenon. Even after such formidable barriers have been overcome, one soon discovers that what is required to gain any degree of mastery is practice, constant practice, and still more practice.

Eventually I overcame the problem, at least to some extent. But my experience prompted me to conclude that there was a need for a manual such as this one. It is designed for students who have completed at least a year or two of Greek, without having learned anything about accents, and who then want to catch up in this area.

There are always students who want to learn as much as possible about what they study. For them, learning is a pleasure; and a learning challenge is to them what the Himalayas are to the rock climber. Like the Himalayas, accents are there. Beyond that, I hope this *Manual* will demonstrate the usefulness of the study of Greek accents for the understanding of many aspects of the language.

Throughout this *Manual* I have talked about 'rules' of accent; but the term can easily be misunderstood. Rules of accent, like rules of grammar, are neither arbitrary decrees enforced by academics with nothing better to do, nor rigid laws akin to the laws of science. Rather, they are classifications established by careful observation, and they change as the language changes.

New Testament Greek differs from classical Greek, as far as accents are concerned, in not a few details; and such differences have occasionally been pointed out in this *Manual*. The examples and exercises are based on the Greek of the New Testament, even though the same phenomena can be found in other Greek documents of the Hellenistic period; for most students are introduced to the literature of that period through the pages of the New Testament.

It is a pleasure to acknowledge my dependence on grammarians whose works I have culled to write this *Manual*. I refer not only to the grammars *per se*, but also to journal essays and specialized monographs on the pronunciation of Greek (e.g. W. Sidney Allen, *Vox Graeca: The Pronunciation of Classical Greek*, Cambridge, 1974; W. B. Stanford, *The Sound of Greek: Studies in the Greek Theory and Practice of Euphony*, Berkeley, 1967). Rev. John Wenham, as always, was most helpful and encouraging. I am also grateful to successive generations of students whose questions have elicited more precision and care than I could otherwise aspire to: the teacher is the most privileged student of all. Finally, I am deeply indebted to Karen Sich, whose skill on a typewriter leaves me quite in awe.

Soli Deo gloria.

D. A. Carson
Trinity Evangelical Divinity School
Deerfield, IL 60015

Background and Preliminary Definitions

Preliminary Definitions

1. The *ultima* is the final syllable of a word; the *penult* is the second last syllable of a word; and the *antepenult* is the third last syllable of a word.

Comment: These definitions are crucial, since rules for Greek accents largely depend on the ending of a word. However, it is obvious that only words of three syllables or more require all three definitions. A monosyllabic word such as τόν has an ultima; it has neither penult nor antepenult. A disyllabic word such as λόγος has an ultima and a penult, but no antepenult. A trisyllabic word such as ἄνθρωπος has all three, as do all longer words (e.g., λαμβάνομαι, εἰσερχόμεθα, etc.).

2. The vowels ε and ο are always considered *short*; the vowels η and ω are always considered *long*. The other vowels, viz. α, ι, and υ, are variously considered *short* or *long*: there are some rules to be learned as we go along, but frequently there is no rule to be applied. In the latter case, whether α, ι or υ is long or short must be learned by careful observation.

3. Diphthongs are always considered *long*, except for αι and οι which are considered *short* when final (i.e., when they are found at the very end of a word). However, this exception for final αι and οι does not hold in the optative mood (see further Lesson 30).

Comment: In English grammars, a long vowel is often distinguished from a short vowel by sound alone: e.g., long ō as in *nōte* versus short ŏ as in *not*. In phonetics, it is more common to label a vowel 'long' if it is held for a relatively long time, and 'short' if it is held for a relatively short time. The two uses of 'long' and 'short' commonly coalesce: in general, a long vowel like ō in *note* is also held longer than a short vowel like ŏ in *not*. For our purposes, however, 'long' and 'short' are not primarily descriptive of distinctive sounds or of relative time for holding a sound, but are defined values regardless of how a vowel is pronounced or how long it is held. These defined values *may* conform to the distinctions in sound we sometimes make between 'long' and 'short': for instance, in modern pronunciation of New Testament Greek, ε and ο, here defined as short, are pronounced as sounds shorter than η and ω, here defined as long. Some would pronounce a short ι as i in *hit*, and a long ι as i in French *pris*. But few make any distinction in sound between a short α and a long α. Moreover, modern speakers of New Testament Greek do not consistently hold a long vowel longer than a short one. All things considered, it is better to understand 'long' and 'short' as defined values, not descriptive values, even though in this book they will often overlap with distinctive pronunciation or with the distinctive length a sound is sustained.

4. A diphthong formed with an iota subscript is always considered long, even when it is final.

Comment: Most such diphthongs are ῳ or ῃ, which might well be considered long anyway because the main vowel is long. However, by this definition the diphthong ᾳ becomes unambiguously long, regardless of its position in a word, and irrespective of the uncertainty surrounding α itself.

5. A syllable containing a long vowel or a long diphthong is long; all others are necessarily short.

Comment: For example, in λόγος, both the ultima and the penult are short. In ἄνθρωπος, the ultima and the antepenult are short, but the penult is long. The diphthong in ἄνθρωποι is short, and therefore the ultima is short; but the same diphthong in ἀνθρώποις is long, and therefore the ultima is long. The ultima in δίκαια (neuter plural) is short; the ultima in δικαίαν is long. However, in these two words, δίκαια (neuter plural) and δικαίαν, the distinction between long ultima and short ultima does not depend on any definition learned so far, since α may be long or short. On the other hand, the ultima in δικαία is unambiguously long: the reason for this will become apparent shortly.

It is not strictly necessary to be able to break up a word into its precise syllables, as long as one thing is kept in mind: in Greek, each word has as many syllables as it has separate vowels or diphthongs: e.g., *κα-τα-λαμ-βαν-ο-μαι, ἑ-αυ-τους, αὐ-των, ἑ-ως*. Whether there are consonants to be read along with each vowel or diphthong is for our purposes immaterial: it is the vowel or diphthong itself which stands at the heart of every Greek syllable.

6. There are three accents in Greek: the acute (´), the circumflex (˜), and the grave (`).

7. A word is called *oxytone* (from *ὀξύς*, fem. *ὀξεῖα*, 'sharp, pointed') if it has an acute accent on the ultima. A word is called *paroxytone* if it has an acute accent on the penult; and *proparoxytone* if it has an acute accent on the antepenult. A word is called *perispomenon* (cf. *περισπωμένη*, from *περισπάω*, 'to draw off from around, to strip off'—but see the comment) when it has a circumflex accent on the ultima; and *properispomenon* when it has a circumflex accent on the penult. A word with no accent on the ultima is called *barytone* (from *βαρύς*, fem. *βαρεῖα*, which, with reference to sound, signifies 'deep' or 'bass').

> *Comment*: In modern usage, the *word*, not the accented syllable, is called oxytone, perispomenon, barytone, or some other technical designation. This is in contrast with Greek literature, which called the *accent itself ὀξεῖα, περισπωμένη,* or *βαρεῖα*. In each case, the noun *προσῳδία* (= 'accent') must be supplied: the *ὀξεῖα προσῳδία* was the acute accent, and the *περισπωμένη προσῳδία* was the circumflex accent (especially the circumflex found on the ultima). The *βαρεῖα προσῳδία*, the 'deep accent', meant that there was no acute and no circumflex, for both of these were pitched higher (cf. the next sections). In the following pages, however, it is the modern usage which concerns us, in which the word itself receives the technical designation, not its accent or accented syllable.

> *Some examples*: *ναός* is oxytone; *νέος* is paroxytone; and *ἄνθρωπος* is proparoxytone. Further, *παθεῖν* is perispomenon, and *δοῦλος* is properispomenon. Three of these words are also barytones, viz. *νέος*, *ἄνθρωπος* and *δοῦλος*. Clearly, a word that is barytone cannot be simultaneously oxytone or perispomenon.

Writing Greek Accents

1. The accent marks are written over the vowel or diphthong of the syllable to be accented.

2. If a diphthong is to be accented, the accent stands over the second vowel, unless the second vowel is an iota subscript.

Examples: οἶκος, αὐτοῖς, αὐτούς; but ᾔδει and αὐτῷ.

3. When a breathing mark and an accent belong to the same vowel, then in cursive script the acute accent or the grave accent is written beside the breathing, just after it; and the circumflex accent is placed just over the breathing. In uncial script, or when breathing and accent belong to a capital letter, they retain the same relative configuration, but are placed just before the relevant letter.

Examples: ἄνθρωπος, ὅλος, οἶκος, ἥν, ἕν; Ἕλλην, Ἔραστος, Αἴγυπτος (although some modern editors prefer Ἄιγυπτος).

4. In crasis (i.e., the contraction of a vowel or diphthong at the end of a word with a vowel or diphthong at the beginning of the following word), the first of the two words always loses its accent.

Examples: καὶ ἐγώ becomes κἀγώ; καὶ ἐκεῖθεν becomes κἀκεῖθεν.

The Historical Significance of Accents

In Greek before the New Testament period, the three accents indicated not stress, but pitch: that is, an accented syllable gained a particular frequency, not a particular volume. A syllable with an acute accent was spoken with a rising pitch: the pitch might rise by a musical fifth. A syllable with a circumflex indicated a pitch that first rose and then fell: a circumflex accent was first perceived as a combination of an acute and a grave (´ ` = ˜). The grave itself might be thought to indicate a falling pitch, but in fact it indicated a pitch maintained at the normal level, in contrast to (and therefore lower than) the acute or the circumflex.

These accents were not written in earliest times, but were developed about 200 B.C. by grammarians who wished to codify the language and help foreigners learn it. Differences in pitch had been *assumed* in the language from ancient times; but now the practice was formulated. The formulation of the category 'grave accent' was awkward in some ways; for if the grave indicated the absence of either an acute or a circumflex, then *every* syllable had to receive an accent mark. We might expect something like this:

ἡ ἀγάπὴ τοῦ θεοῦ

With time, however, because grave accents indicated only the absence of the other two, they were dropped entirely, except for one particular usage which will be discussed in the General Rules found in the next lesson. The same Greek phrase therefore came to be written like this:

$$\dot{\eta} \; \dot{\alpha}\gamma\dot{\alpha}\pi\eta \; \tauο\tilde{υ} \; θεο\tilde{υ}$$

It is very difficult for modern English speakers to pronounce Greek accents in terms of musical pitch. To be sure, we use pitch in English; but it is used idiosyncratically, changing somewhat from speaker to speaker, and according to the shade of meaning intended. We distinguish, for instance, the emphatic 'Yés!', the open but questioning 'Yè-és?', and the doubtful and perhaps ironic 'Yé-ès'. In Greek of the period before the New Testament, however, the tonal system was a fixed part of the language and helped to establish the essential meaning, just as varied pitch helps to establish meaning in Chinese. Many grammarians repeat the story of the actor Hegelochus who, when quoting a line from Euripides ending in γαλήν ' ὁρῶ ('I see a calm'), pronounced a circumflex accent instead of the acute, and brought the house down: γαλῆν ὁρῶ means 'I see a weasel'.

If accents indicate pitch, then they are independent of stress. Hence, in a word like παρουσία, the long vowel sound of the diphthong ου may be stressed, while the accented ί receives a rising pitch. Is this what we should attempt?

Unfortunately, the problem is yet more complicated. By the fourth century A.D. it is clear that accents no longer reflect pitch, but stress. This signals a major change in pronunciation. At that late date, a word like παρουσία must be stressed on the accented ί, not on the long vowel sound of the diphthong. The question that concerns us, then, is when this change from pitch accents to stress accents occurred. More precisely, did the New Testament writers pronounce Greek using musical pitch or stress?

This question is extraordinarily difficult to answer. There is still no consensus, although the majority now incline to the latter view. But then we must ask how the modern student of New Testament Greek ought to pronounce these accents. And again there is no consensus. A very small number of purists try to teach their students musical pitch. The vast majority, however, follow one of three practices: (1) they leave out virtually all accents; (2) they write the accents in but do not try to pronounce them: i.e., they pronounce the words as they see fit, often but not invariably stressing the long vowel, and not attempting to reflect the accents in pronunciation; or (3) they treat the accents as markers of stress, not pitch, and rigorously stress every syllable with an accent of whatever sort.

To teach students of New Testament Greek to pronounce the accents according to pitch is not practicable. For a start, too few of us who teach could do an acceptable job! Moreover, in the charged curricula of modern undergraduate and graduate institutions, I doubt that there is enough time. After all, most of our students do not intend to major in the Greek language, but merely study it enough to use it with reasonable competence. Of the three major alternatives, I have questioned the first in the Preface to this book, and need not repeat myself. The second alternative is defensible enough; and students who follow that route will find this book useful in writing Greek accents, even if they choose not to pronounce them. But pedagogically speaking, I have found the third alternative the best, for it forces the attention of the student on the Greek accents he is reading, and thereby assists the student's memory. Moreover, this third alternative introduces uniformity of pronunciation into reading, and this enables students reading aloud to understand and reinforce each other more quickly than is otherwise the case.

In Lesson 37, I shall again raise the vexed question of the practice of the New Testament writers themselves. My own practice is to stress all Greek accents; and I recommend the practice to students. But this *Manual* does not depend on such advice, which may be cheerfully ignored without loss.

Exercise

Thoroughly memorize the definitions in this chapter.

The General Rules of Accent

GR.1 Apart from specific exceptions later to be enumerated, every Greek word must have an accent, but only one accent.

Comment: The exceptions largely concern enclitics and proclitics, discussed in Lesson 9. But see also the observations on crasis in Lesson 1, and on elision in Lesson 7.

GR.2 An acute accent may stand only on an ultima, a penult, or an antepenult; a circumflex accent may stand only on an ultima or a penult; and a grave accent may stand only on an ultima.

Comment: It follows that ἄνθρωπος and ἀνθρῶπος are impossible. Similarly ἄποστολος must be excluded. One could not at this juncture exclude ἀπόστολος, nor ἀποστολὸς.

GR.3 The circumflex accent cannot stand on a short syllable.

Comment: Hence, although ἀποστόλος is not excluded by *GR.2*, it is excluded by *GR.3*.

GR.4 If the ultima is long, then:

> **GR.4.1** the antepenult cannot have any accent, and
> **GR.4.2** the penult, if it is accented at all, must have the acute.

Comment: This rule constitutes a limitation on *GR.2*. Under the stipulated condition—that the ultima is long—the acute accent becomes restricted to the ultima and the penult, and the circumflex accent becomes

restricted to the ultima. Thus, although ἀπόστολος is possible, ἀπόσ-
τολου is not; and although δοῦλος is possible, δοῦλου is not. Note
carefully that *GR.4.2* does not *require* that the penult take the acute
when the ultima is long. Rather, it stipulates that if the ultima is long
and if the penult is accented at all, the accent on that penult must be an
acute accent. The rule, therefore, does not violate θεοῦ.

GR.5 If the ultima is short, then a long penult, if it is accented at all, must
have the circumflex accent.

Comment: Observe that this rule does not *require* that a long penult
succeeded by a short ultima take the circumflex accent. Rather, if the
ultima is short and the penult is long, then the penult, *if it is accented*,
must have the circumflex accent. The rule would be violated by δούλος
and by δούλοι; but it is not violated by δούλου, θεῶν, or υἱός.

GR.6 An acute accent on the ultima of a word is changed to a grave when
followed, without intervening mark of punctuation, by another word
or words.

Comment: The correct accentuation of the Greek word 'son' in the
nominative case is as follows: υἱός. In the Greek expression 'the son of
man', however, the acute accent on υἱός is changed to a grave accent: ὁ
υἱὸς τοῦ ἀνθρώπου.

Clearly, it is the ultima which of all syllables allows the greatest diversity
of accentuation. If it is short, it can take an acute accent or a grave accent
(as in the two examples just given, respectively); and if it is long, it can take
an acute accent (e.g., οὐδείς), a circumflex accent (e.g., θεοῦ), or a grave
accent (e.g., οὐδεὶς ἑώρακεν θεόν).
Words which end with the grave accent because of *GR.6* must not be
confused with barytones (which, it will be remembered, have no accent at
all on the ultima). In fact, words with a grave accent on the ultima are
considered to be oxytones, since such words in isolation would have the
acute accent on the ultima were it not for the flow of words. Hence, even in
the expression ὁ υἱὸς τοῦ ἀνθρώπου, the word υἱός is oxytone. These
distinctions will serve us well when we come to Lesson 9.
The General Rules do not usually determine what syllable must be
accented and what accent that syllable must have. On the contrary: they are
by and large concerned with what *cannot* be done, rather than with what
must be done. For instance, the General Rules permit δίκαιος, δικαῖος,
and δικαιός, even though only the first is correct; but the Rules exclude
such things as δῖκαιος (*GR.2*; *GR.3*), δικαίος (*GR.5*), δικαιὸς (*GR.3*), and

δικαὶος (*GR.2*). In short, the General Rules provide a framework within
which to operate; but in order to learn exactly where an accent must
be placed, and what kind of accent it must be, other rules must be brought
to bear.

Exercise

Thoroughly memorize the General Rules, and then answer the following:

1. Explain what is wrong with the accentuation of the following Greek
   words, giving as many reasons as possible.

ἀποστολὸς	*πρῶτος*
ἁποστολος	*ὁ υἱός τοῦ ἄνθρωπου*
Χρῖστου	*ἀνθρῶπῳ*
Ἰῆσους	*θε͂ος*
θὲου	

2. Only one of each pair of words in the following list is correct. Choose
   the correct word and justify your answer.

δίκαιος	or	*δικαίος*
ἄνθρωποις	or	*ἀνθρώποις*
δούλῳ	or	*δοῦλῳ*
αὐτῳ	or	*αὐτῷ*
σκοτὶα	or	*σκοτία*

LESSON **3**

The Basic Rule for Verbs

The basic rule for verbs may be stated as follows:

VR.1 The accent in finite verbal forms is recessive.

> *Comment*: This is an immensely powerful rule, one which definitely fixes the accent on all words to which the rule applies. An accent is *recessive* if it is placed as far back from the end of the word as the General Rules permit. This rule applies to 'finite verbal forms': i.e., infinitives and participles are explicitly excluded from the rule.

In practice, this recessive rule fixes not only the syllable which must be accented, but the kind of accent to be applied. The General Rules turn out to be sufficiently detailed that there is never any ambiguity in this regard.

For example, consider ἐπιγινωσκομεν. *GR.2* guarantees that the required accent cannot be placed farther back than the ω. On the other hand, there is nothing to prevent an accent on this syllable. Although the syllable is long, nevertheless because it is the antepenult, both the circumflex accent and the grave accent are excluded (*GR.2*). Therefore the only possible accentuation of this verb is ἐπιγινώσκομεν.

Consider σωζε. The recessive rule guarantees that the accent will in this instance be placed on the penult, not the ultima; and *GR.5* insists that the accent will be the circumflex: σῶζε.

By the application of this recessive rule, the accents on the present indicative active of the paradigm verb λύω are completely determined:

$$λύω$$
$$λύεις$$
$$λύει$$
$$λύομεν$$
$$λύετε$$
$$λύουσιν$$

Because accent rules are based on the *endings* of words, therefore all verbs with these *endings* can be expected to follow the same pattern of accents, viz. an acute on the final syllable of the stem. For instance:

βάλλω	γινώσκω	ἐσθίω
βάλλεις	γινώσκεις	ἐσθίεις
βάλλει	γινώσκει	ἐσθίει
βάλλομεν	γινώσκομεν	ἐσθίομεν
βάλλετε	γινώσκετε	ἐσθίετε
βάλλουσιν	γινώσκουσιν	ἐσθίουσιν

This recessive rule can in principle be applied to any tense, any mood, and any voice. Only the non-finite forms of verbs are systematically excluded from the rule. However, because there are many subtle exceptions and adaptations, even on forms to which the rule applies, it is best to restrict the exercises to present tense verbs in the indicative mood, active voice, until such exceptions and adaptations are explained.

Exercise

Correctly accent the following forms:

1. λαμβανετε
2. ἐγειρω
3. ἐχεις
4. θεραπευουσιν
5. μενει
6. πεμπουσιν
7. κρινετε
8. ἐσθιεις
9. εὑρισκομεν
10. σωζει

LESSON **4**

Contract Verbs

VR.2 In contract verbs, if either of the contracting syllables, before contraction, has an accent, then the resulting contracted syllable has an accent.

> **VR.2.1** If the resulting contracted syllable is a penult or an antepenult, and has an accent, the General Rules always tell what kind of accent it will be.
>
> **VR.2.2** If the resulting contracted syllable is an ultima, and has an accent, the accent must be a circumflex.

Comment: The basic verb rule, *VR.1*, is presupposed, and applied to the uncontracted form of the verb: e.g., φιλε+ομεν, according to *VR.1*, must be accented thus: φιλέ+ομεν. In other words, one of the contracting syllables, before contraction, is being accented; and therefore the contracted syllable must have an accent (*VR.2*): i.e., in φιλουμεν, the ου must have an accent. *VR.2.1* tells us to apply the General Rules to ου; and the result is φιλοῦμεν.

Consider ἐφιλε+ον. Application of the basic recessive rule yields ἐφίλε+ον. Neither of the contracting syllables has an accent; and therefore *VR.2* does not apply. In the contracted form of the verb, the accent therefore stays where it is: ἐφίλουν.

Consider φιλε+ω. Application of the recessive rule yields φιλέ+ω. One of the contracting syllables has an accent; and therefore the contracted syllable ω in φιλω must have an accent. The contracted syllable is an ultima, so *VR.2.2* applies: φιλῶ.

There is another way of looking at accented and contracting syllables. When all the possibilities of *VR.2*, *VR.2.1* and *VR.2.2* are explored, one discovers that: (a) if the first of the two contracting syllables, before contraction, has the acute, then the acute combines with the unwritten grave accent (cf. Lesson 1) on the other contracting syllable to form the circumflex: e.g., $\varphi\iota\lambda\acute{\epsilon}+\omega = \varphi\iota\lambda\acute{\epsilon}+\grave{\omega} \rightarrow \varphi\iota\lambda\acute{\grave{\omega}} = \varphi\iota\lambda\tilde{\omega}$; and (b) if the second of two contracting syllables, before contraction, has the acute accent, then the contracted syllable also has the acute, since clearly ` ´ will not combine to generate ´` = ~: e.g., $\varphi\iota\lambda\epsilon+\acute{o}\mu\epsilon\theta\alpha = \varphi\grave{\iota}\lambda\grave{\epsilon}+\acute{o}\mu\grave{\epsilon}\theta\grave{\alpha} \rightarrow \varphi\iota\lambda o\grave{\upsilon}\mu\grave{\epsilon}\theta\grave{\alpha} = \varphi\iota\lambda o\acute{\upsilon}\mu\epsilon\theta\alpha$.

By such means, we may deduce the correct accentuation of the present indicative active of $\varphi\iota\lambda\acute{\epsilon}\omega$:

$\varphi\iota\lambda\acute{\epsilon}+\omega \rightarrow \varphi\iota\lambda\tilde{\omega}$
$\varphi\iota\lambda\acute{\epsilon}+\epsilon\iota\varsigma \rightarrow \varphi\iota\lambda\epsilon\tilde{\iota}\varsigma$
$\varphi\iota\lambda\acute{\epsilon}+\epsilon\iota \rightarrow \varphi\iota\lambda\epsilon\tilde{\iota}$
$\varphi\iota\lambda\acute{\epsilon}+o\mu\epsilon\nu \rightarrow \varphi\iota\lambda o\tilde{\upsilon}\mu\epsilon\nu$
$\varphi\iota\lambda\acute{\epsilon}+\epsilon\tau\epsilon \rightarrow \varphi\iota\lambda\epsilon\tilde{\iota}\tau\epsilon$
$\varphi\iota\lambda\acute{\epsilon}+o\upsilon\sigma\iota\nu \rightarrow \varphi\iota\lambda o\tilde{\upsilon}\sigma\iota\nu$

Of course, it is easy enough to figure this out from first principles, as we have done. But it is helpful to observe and memorize the resulting pattern of accents: in the present active indicative of contract verbs, there is a circumflex on the first syllable of the inflected suffix all through the conjugation. Naturally, this turns out to be the invariable pattern. For instance:

αἰτῶ	θεωρῶ	μετανοῶ
αἰτεῖς	θεωρεῖς	μετανοεῖς
αἰτεῖ	θεωρεῖ	μετανοεῖ
αἰτοῦμεν	θεωροῦμεν	μετανοοῦμεν
αἰτεῖτε	θεωρεῖτε	μετανοεῖτε
αἰτοῦσιν	θεωροῦσιν	μετανοοῦσιν

In comparing this paradigm with the $\lambda\acute{\upsilon}\omega$ paradigm of the last lesson, it becomes clear that as far as accents are concerned the two are quite distinct. Indeed, in the present active indicative, only the accent distinguishes an -εω contract verb from a non-contract verb in all but two instances (the first and second person plural).

The rules for contract verbs, here applied to -εω contracts, apply equally to -οω and -αω contracts; and they apply to tense/voice/mood combinations other than the present active indicative. However, because adaptations are sometimes required, it is best to practice first on the present active indicative of -εω contracts.

In their uncontracted state (the way they appear in the lexica) -εω contract verbs in the first person singular, present indicative active, will always have an acute on the penult ε: e.g., αἰτέω, βλασφημέω, εὐλογέω, etc.

Exercise

Correctly accent the following forms:

1. λαλουμεν
2. ποιουσιν
3. θεραπευει
4. καλεις
5. μισω
6. αἰτει
7. ζητειτε
8. φιλουμεν
9. μαρτυρουσιν
10. τηρει

LESSON **5**

The Basic Rule for Nouns; Nouns of the First and Second Declensions

The basic rule for nouns may be stated as follows:

NR.1 In nouns, the accent remains on the same syllable as in the nominative singular, as nearly as the General Rules and certain specific exceptions (*NR.5* and *NR.11*) will permit.

Comment: This rule differs enormously from the basic verb rule (*VR.1*), in that it fixes nothing. *Accents on nouns must therefore be memorized as part of the spelling of the nominative singular.* What the noun rule guarantees, however, is that if one knows the accent of a noun when that noun is in both the nominative case and the singular number (which of course are the case and number of nouns as they are memorized), one is able to deduce the accent on that noun throughout its declension. Whatever ambiguities may arise are resolved by subsequent rules.

Consider ἄνθρωπος. If we do not know the correct accent for this word in the nominative singular, there is nothing to help us but a lexicon. Once we see that the word is correctly accented on the antepenult, ἄνθρωπος, we can deduce what accent must be on ἀνθρώπου. The long ultima excludes the possibility of any accent remaining on the antepenult (*GR.4.1*); but the penult can have an accent, and *GR.4.2* requires that the accent be an acute. Hence ἀνθρώπου.

Consider δοῦλος. In the plural nominative, there is no reason why we cannot retain the accent as it is in the singular nominative: hence δοῦλοι. However in any case with a long ultima, such as the genitive plural δούλων,

27

the accent for the word can no longer be a circumflex on the penult
(*GR.4.2*). On the other hand, there is nothing in the General Rules to
forbid that *any* accent be placed on the penult under these conditions, so
there is no necessity to move the accent from the penult to the ultima. All
we need to do is change the circumflex accent on the penult to an acute
accent on the penult. Hence δούλων.

A plethora of examples would show us very quickly that, once the
accent of a noun in the nominative singular is known, the basic noun rule
definitely fixes the accent for the other declined forms of that noun,
provided the noun is barytone. If, however, there is an accent on the ultima
of a noun in the nominative singular (i.e., the noun is not barytone), then a
new ambiguity arises. For example, consider ὁδός. Lengthening the ultima
cannot move the accent to another syllable; but what accent should be
applied? When the ultima is short (as in ὁδός, ὁδέ, ὁδόν, and ὁδοί), then
the accent must be acute (or grave when followed by other words, *GR.6*)
and not circumflex, because the circumflex accent cannot stand on a short
syllable (*GR.3*). But what about forms with a long syllable? Should we
adopt ὁδού, ὁδῷ, ὁδούς, ὁδών and ὁδοίς, or alternatively ὁδοῦ, ὁδῷ, ὁδοῦς,
ὁδῶν and ὁδοῖς—or some combination? The noun rule *NR.1* does not
specify, and another is needed.

NR.2 In both the first and second declensions, when the ultima takes an
acute accent in the nominative singular, it has the circumflex accent
in the genitives and datives of both numbers, and elsewhere the acute
accent.

Comment: This rule will affect all oxytone nouns of the first and
second declensions (e.g., ὁδός, υἱός, θεός, γραφή, ἀρχή, γενεά, μαθητής,
κριτής, ἱερόν), but nothing else, because the rule is applicable only to
first and second declension nouns where 'the *ultima* is accented'. In
effect, the rule tells us when oxytone nouns of the first and second
declensions become perispomenon. The phrase 'elsewhere the acute
accent' really refers, in the *second* declension, only to the accusative
plural, for only in the accusative plural is there a long vowel or diphthong
capable of sustaining a circumflex. The nominative singular, vocative
singular, accusative singular, nominative plural, and vocative plural, all
have a short ultima which automatically precludes a circumflex accent
(*GR.3*). Hence in the forms of ὁδός with a long ultima, listed above, the
correct accentuation is: ὁδοῦ, ὁδῷ, ὁδούς, ὁδῶν, ὁδοῖς.

The phrase 'elsewhere the acute accent' potentially refers in the *first*
declension to any form outside the genitive and datives of both numbers,

because in that declension long ultimas can appear throughout the declensions of oxytone words: e.g., μαθητής, γραφή. Full examples will be provided in the next chapter.

Here, then, are some sample nouns from the second declension which make full use of *NR.1* and *NR.2*:

Sing. N.	ἀπόστολος	λόγος	Ἰουδαῖος	λαός
V.	ἀπόστολε	λόγε	Ἰουδαῖε	λαέ
A.	ἀπόστολον	λόγον	Ἰουδαῖον	λαόν
G.	ἀποστόλου	λόγου	Ἰουδαίου	λαοῦ
D.	ἀποστόλῳ	λόγῳ	Ἰουδαίῳ	λαῷ
Plur. N.V.	ἀπόστολοι	λόγοι	Ἰουδαῖοι	λαοί
A.	ἀποστόλους	λόγους	Ἰουδαίους	λαούς
G.	ἀποστόλων	λόγων	Ἰουδαίων	λαῶν
D.	ἀποστόλοις	λόγοις	Ἰουδαίοις	λαοῖς

When the verb rules are studied, it is not necessary to provide lists of verbs with accents in the first person singular, because the verb recessive rule is powerful enough to fix the accent. This is not the case with nouns: the accent must be learned with each word in the nominative singular. For the time being, I shall provide lists with which to work; but later in the *Manual*, the student may need to check where the accent goes on a particular noun (in the nominative singular) by consulting a lexicon.

This first list is made up of nouns from the (usually) masculine gender of the second declension:

ἄγγελος	θρόνος	ὀφθαλμός
ἀγρός	Ἰουδαῖος	παραλυτικός
ἀδελφός	κόσμος	ποταμός
ἄνθρωπος	κύριος	πρεσβύτερος
ἀπόστολος	λαός	τόπος
διάκονος	λεπρός	Φαρισαῖος
διδάσκαλος	λίθος	φίλος
ἐχθρός	λόγος	φόβος
θάνατος	νόμος	Χριστός

To these we may add three indeclinable words, in order to increase the stock of words whose accents we know. Indeclinable words are discussed more fully in Lesson 7. For now it is sufficient to note the accent, and to observe that the General Rules must still be observed.

Ἰσραήλ
καί
ὦ (interjection, exclamation: often in direct address)

Exercise A

Correctly accent the following sentences:

1. ἀποστολος θεραπευει παραλυτικον;
2. Χριστος κρινει ἀνθρωπους και ἀγγελους.
3. μαρτυρουμεν και λαος μετανοει.
4. ὠ Ἰσραηλ, θανατον ζητειτε;
5. ἀποστολοι λαλουσιν και διακονοι ἐχουσιν φοβον.
6. φοβος λαμβανει ἀδελφους και λαον.
7. ἀδελφος ἐχει ἀγρον.
8. κυριοι πεμπουσιν ἀγγελους και λογους γραφουσιν.
9. Ἰουδαιοι και Φαρισαιοι αἰτουσιν φιλους.
10. μισει κοσμον και ζητει φιλον.

Without adding further rules, we may note an important extension of the established rules. Because the masculine article is essentially patterned after the second declension of nouns, the same accent rules apply, with but two exceptions. Hence:

Sing. N.	ὁ
A.	τόν
G.	τοῦ
D.	τῷ
Plur. N.	οἱ
A.	τούς
G.	τῶν
D.	τοῖς

The two exceptions are the nominative singular form and the nominative plural form, ὁ and οἱ respectively. These forms, called *proclitics* (cf. Lesson 9), are almost never accented.

One of the most commonly used *irregular* second declension masculine nouns, the Greek word for 'Jesus', is irregular not only in inflection but also, it appears, in accent:

N.	Ἰησοῦς
V.	Ἰησοῦ
A.	Ἰησοῦν
G.	Ἰησοῦ
D.	Ἰησοῦ

Because of *NR.2*, it is surprising to find a circumflex on an ultima other than in the genitive and dative cases. But a further rule covers this and similar exceptions:

NR.3 In both the first and second declensions, when the ultima in the nominative singular has a circumflex accent, the circumflex accent remains on the ultima in all the singular forms.

Comment: In the New Testament this rule is only rarely applied. Another example is found in the next chapter.

Here are more second declension masculine nouns in the nominative singular, the accentuation of which must be memorized:

ἁμαρτωλός	Ἰάκωβος	ὄχλος
ἄνεμος	καρπός	παρθένος
ἄρτος	μισθός	πειρασμόν
διάβολος	ναός	σταυρός
δοῦλος	ὁδός	υἱός
ἔρημος	οἶκος	καιρός
ἥλιος	οἶνος	χρόνος
θεός	οὐρανός	

To this we may add one more word, just because it is so common: ἐστίν. The accent rules surrounding this word are notoriously difficult, and will not be discussed in detail until Lesson 9. For the time being, we shall dangerously simplify the relevant rules and say that the word should be accented ἔστιν when it is first in its clause, and ἐστίν elsewhere (unless, of course, under the condition of *GR.6*, it becomes ἐστίν).

Exercise B

Correctly accent the following sentences:

1. οἱ δουλοι ποιουσιν ὁδον τω κυριω.
2. μετανοουσιν και μισουσιν πειρασμον.
3. ὁ Ἰησους εὐλογει τον ἀρτον και τον οἰνον του ἐχθρου.
4. ἀνθρωπος και διακονος λαμβανουσιν τον καρπον του πρεσβυτερου.
5. ὁ ἡλιος και ὁ ἀνεμος θεραπευουσιν.
6. ὁ υἱος του θεου ζητει τους οὐρανους;
7. παρθενοι γινωσκουσιν τους λογους του ὀχλου.
8. ὁ ἀγγελος γραφει νομους τω κοσμω.
9. ὁ διαβολος μισει τον του θεου ναον.
10. ὁ Κυριος σωζει ἁμαρτωλους.

Second Declension Neuter Nouns; First Declension Feminine Nouns; The Definite Article

The noun rules covered so far apply without difficulty to second declension neuter nouns. For instance:

Sing. N.V.	ἔργον	πρόβατον	πλοῖον	ἱερόν
A.	ἔργον	πρόβατον	πλοῖον	ἱερόν
G.	ἔργου	προβάτου	πλοίου	ἱεροῦ
D.	ἔργῳ	προβάτῳ	πλοίῳ	ἱερῷ
Plur. N.	ἔργα	πρόβατα	πλοῖα	ἱερά
A.	ἔργα	πρόβατα	πλοῖα	ἱερά
G.	ἔργων	προβάτων	πλοίων	ἱερῶν
D.	ἔργοις	προβάτοις	πλοίοις	ἱεροῖς

Almost all of these forms are deducible from *NR.1* and *NR.2*, once the correct accent of the nominative singular of each word is known. One detail, however, could not be deduced from *NR.1* and *NR.2*, and therefore merits special notice: the final *a* in the plural nominative and accusative is considered short, or else πρόβατα could not be proparoxytone, nor πλοῖα properispomenon (*GR.4*). This leads us to formulate one further rule:

NR.4 The *a* in the ultima of nominative and accusative plural neuter nouns is always considered short.

In principle, this rule, in addition to those already enunciated, enables the student to handle all second declension neuter nouns. As we shall see (Lesson 21), the rule applies to all neuter nouns, including those of the *third* declension. It does not apply to nouns ending in *a* which are not neuter, and therefore does not affect the first declension (cf. *NR.6*; *NR.7*; *NR.8*).

Feminine first declension nouns, however, in addition to following *NR.1*, *NR.2*, and *NR.3* (Lesson 5), require four extra rules.

NR.5 In the first declension only, the genitive plural exhibits an exception to the basic noun rule (*NR.1*); the genitive plural *must* have a circumflex accent on the ultima regardless of where the accent falls in the nominative singular.

Comment: This rule applies to all nouns in the first declension, not just those of the feminine gender. Hence, the first declension masculine nouns to be studied in the next lesson follow this rule. The rule does not really come into force when the word is an oxytone or a perispomenon in the nominative singular. For instance, in the declension of ἀρχή, *NR.1* and *NR.2* alone are sufficient to explain all the accents, including the circumflex on the genitive plural:

Sing. N.V.	ἀρχή
A.	ἀρχήν
G.	ἀρχῆς
D.	ἀρχῇ
Plur. N.V.	ἀρχαί
A.	ἀρχάς
G.	ἀρχῶν
D.	ἀρχαῖς

If the first declension noun is other than an oxytone or a perispomenon, however, *NR.5* comes into play. For example:

Sing. N.V.	διαθήκη
A.	διαθήκην
G.	διαθήκης
D.	διαθήκῃ
Plur. N.V.	διαθῆκαι
A.	διαθήκας
G.	διαθηκῶν
D.	διαθήκαις

To decline διαθήκη is to reveal another ambiguity: is the α in the final syllable of the accusative plural short or long? Clearly it is here reckoned long, or else the correct accentuation would be διαθῆκας, not, as is the case, διαθήκας. In fact we may establish this as a rule:

NR.6 The *a* in the ultima of all first declension accusative plural nouns is always considered long.

A further point must be clarified. Feminine first declension nouns are of three types: those which in the nominative singular end in *η* (as *ἀρχή* and *διαθήκη, supra*); those which in the nominative singular end in *a* and whose stems end in a vowel or *ρ* (e.g., *ἡμέρα*); and those which in the nominative singular end in *a* but whose stems end in a consonant other than *ρ* (e.g., *δόξα*). The latter two types raise extra questions in the singular forms because of the ambiguity surrounding *a*: is it long or short? (There are no additional questions in the plural forms because there is only one set of plural case endings throughout the first declension: cf. *ἀρχή* and *διαθήκη, supra*.)

Consider the following examples of the second and third types respectively:

Sing. **N.V.**	*ἡμέρα*	*δόξα*
A.	*ἡμέραν*	*δόξαν*
G.	*ἡμέρας*	*δόξης*
D.	*ἡμέρᾳ*	*δόξῃ*

One cannot tell if the *a* in the ultimas of six of these forms is long or short; but clearly it would make a difference to the accentuation of the word if that word were a proparoxytone or a properispomenon. The following two rules remove the ambiguity:

NR.7 In first declension nouns ending in *a* or *aς*, whether the *a* in the ultima is long or short in the nominative singular, it is the same in the vocative and the accusative singular.

Comment: Consider *ἀλήθεια*. The ultima must be short: the antepenult has an accent (*GR.2*). Therefore the correct accent of the accusative singular is *ἀλήθειαν*. Similarly for *γλῶσσα, γλῶσσαν*. On the other hand, in *βασιλεία*, the ultima must be long, or else the long penult would have the circumflex accent (*GR.5*). Therefore the correct accent for the accusative singular is *βασιλείαν*. Similarly for *ὥρα, ὥραν*. In instances where one cannot tell from the nominative singular whether the ultima is long or short, the same ambiguity is nicely preserved in the accusative singular: e.g., *σωτηρία,* or *παρουσία*, where, if the *ι* is long, so must be the *a*; but if the *ι* is short, we cannot judge whether the *a* is long or short. In any case we cannot get by the first step and learn at a glance whether the *ι* is long or short; but this rule shows we do not need to.

The rule treats first declension nouns ending in ας as well as those ending in α. The former condition applies to *masculine* first declension nouns, discussed later (Lesson 7).

Unfortunately, no rule completely resolves the accents on the nominative singular declensional forms of words such as θύρα and ἐργάτης. Is the penult long or short? If long, then the ultima of θύρα is also long, or else the word would be accented θῦρα (cf. *GR.4*; *GR.5*). *NR.7*, as we have seen, neatly resolves the accusative singular; but the nominative plural remains untouched. If the penult in either θύρα or ἐργάτης is long, then in the nominative singular the accent must be circumflex: θῦραι and ἐργᾶται. In fact, the penult is short, and the correct accent in both instances is acute: θύραι and ἐργάται. But no rule predicts this. The uncertainty exists only for first declension paroxytones ending in α or ας, and only in the nominative plural. Most of the crucial penults are short; but short or long, the accent on the nominative plural must be learned by inspection.

NR.8 The α in the ultima of first declension feminine nouns is considered long when it occurs in the singular genitive and dative.

Comment: The correct declensional forms of ἀλήθεια and μετάνοια, therefore, are as follows:

Sing. N.V.	ἀλήθεια	μετάνοια
A.	ἀλήθειαν	μετάνοιαν
G.	ἀληθείας	μετανοίας
D.	ἀληθείᾳ	μετανοίᾳ

Words such as βασιλεία and ὥρα will not, of course, be affected. Moreover, words such as δόξα are unaffected by this rule, because feminine first declension nouns in α whose stems end in a consonant other than ρ take η in the genitive singular and dative singular.

The accents on the full declension of the article, based as they are on first and second declension nouns, follow as a matter of course (apart from the four unaccented words, *proclitics*, which must be carefully noted):

Sing. N.	ὁ	ἡ	τό
A.	τόν	τήν	τό
G.	τῶν	τῆς	τοῦ
D.	τῷ	τῇ	τῷ
Plur. N.	οἱ	αἱ	τά
A.	τούς	τάς	τά
G.	τῶν	τῶν	τῶν
D.	τοῖς	ταῖς	τοῖς

One final point. In the last lesson, *NR.3* dealt with nouns of the first and second declension which have a circumflex accent on the nominative singular. That will not occur often in the second declension, where nouns in the nominative singular normally end in -*ος* or -*ον*, and therefore preclude the possibility of a circumflex on the ultima (*GR.3*). The only example provided was the *irregular* second declension word, Ἰησοῦς. In theory it could occur more often in the first declension, where long ultimas are common; but it is still very rare. One important example, however, is:

Sing. N.V.	γῆ
A.	γῆν
G.	γῆς
D.	γῇ

The word appears about 240 times in the Greek New Testament, and, like Ἰησοῦς, only in the singular.

Again, it is worth providing correctly accented vocabulary in progressive steps, and corresponding exercises:

ἀργύριον	ἱμάτιον	πρόβατον
βιβλίον	μνημεῖον	πρόσωπον
δαιμόνιον	μυστήριον	σημεῖον
δένδρον	παιδίον	συνέδριον
ἔργον	τέκνον	σάββατον
εὐαγγέλιον	πλοῖον	(τὰ) Ἱεροσόλυμα
ἱερόν	ποτήριον	

To this we may add a further indeclinable word (cf. Lesson 7): (ἡ) Ἱερουσαλήμ.

Exercise A

1. *οἱ ἀπόστολοι λαλουσιν το εὐαγγελιον κυριοις και δουλοις.*
2. *τα τεκνα αἰτει τους πρεσβυτερους ἱματια.*
3. *ἀγγελοι θεωρουσιν το προσωπον του θεου.*
4. *οἱ ἀνθρωποι ἐχουσιν προβατα και πλοιον.*
5. *βλεπομεν τα σημεια των καιρων.*
6. *το σαββατον του θεου σημειον ἐστιν.*
7. *Χριστος εὐλογει το ποτηριον οἰνου και τον ἀρτον.*
8. *οἱ διακονοι τηρουσιν τα ποτηρια του ἱερου Ἱεροσολυμων.*
9. *τα δαιμονια φιλει τα μνημεια.*
10. *οἱ Φαρισαιοι του συνεδριου ποιουσιν ἱματιον τῳ Ἰησου;*

Further correctly accented vocabulary:

ἀγάπη	ἐντολή	προσευχή
ἀρχή	ἐπιστολή	συναγωγή
γῆ	ζωή	τιμή
γραφή	κεφαλή	ὑπομονή
διαθήκη	κώμη	φυλακή
διδαχή	νεφέλη	φωνή
δικαιοσύνη	ὀργή	ψυχή
εἰρήνη	παραβολή	

Exercise B

1. γινωσκουσιν οἱ ἀδελφοι την ἀγαπην του θεου.
2. τα δαιμονια φιλει την του θεου διαθηκην;
3. εὐλογουμεν την ὑπομονην του Χριστου.
4. τα τεκνα λαμβανει τα βιβλια της γραφης;
5. ὁ Ἰησους λαλει τας παραβολας τῳ λαῳ της κωμης.
6. πεμπεις τους λογους του εὐαγγελιου της εἰρηνης.
7. ἐσθιομεν τον καρπον της γης.
8. οἱ δουλοι μισουσιν την φυλακην.
9. οἱ ἀποστολοι ἐχουσιν την τιμην των ἀνθρωπων.
10. ὁ Ἰακωβος πεμπει ἐπιστολην τῳ φιλῳ του ἀποστολου.

Further correctly accented vocabulary:

ἀδικία	ἐπαγγελία	παρουσία
ἀλήθεια	ἡμέρα	πέτρα
ἁμαρτία	θάλασσα	σοφία
βασιλεία	θύρα	σωτηρία
Γαλιλαία	θυσία	χαρά
γενεά	Ἰουδαία	χήρα
γλῶσσα	καρδία	χρεία
δόξα	μαρτυρία	ὥρα
ἐκκλησία	μετάνοια	Παῦλος
ἐξουσία	οἰκία	Πέτρος

Exercise C

1. ὁ θεος μισει την ἀδικιαν και την ἁμαρτιαν.
2. ἡ μετανοια θυρα της σωτηριας ἐστιν.
3. ἡ γενεα ἁμαρτωλων μετανοει;
4. ζητουσιν τον καιρον της ἐπαγγελιας.
5. θεωρουμεν την ἀρχην της ἡμερας.

6. Χριστος ἐχει την ἐξουσιαν του θεου.
7. Πετρος εὐλογει τον Κυριον της γης και της θαλασσης.
8. ὁ Ἰησους θεραπευει τον υἱον της χηρας.
9. ἡ ὡρα της δοξης του Χριστου χαρα ἐστιν τοις ἀγγελοις.
10. Παυλος ζητει καρδιαν της εἰρηνης και της δικαιοσυνης.

First Declension Masculine Nouns;
Indeclinable Words

First Declension Masculine Nouns

The rules governing the accentuation of first declension masculine nouns have largely been laid down already, in the form of rules for all nouns regardless of declension (*NR.1*), rules for nouns of the first and second declensions (*NR.2*; *NR.3*), and rules for nouns of the first declension (*NR.5*; *NR.6*; *NR.7*). One further rule and several explanatory comments are needed to avoid any residual ambiguity.

NR.9 The final *α* in the vocative of first declension masculine nouns is considered short, unless there is a long *-ας* ultima in the nominative singular, in which instance it is long.

Comments: Compare the following declensional forms:

Sing. **N.**	προφήτης	βαπτιστής	Σατανᾶς	Ἰούδας
V.	προφῆτα	βαπτιστά	Σατανᾶ	Ἰούδα
A.	προφήτην	βαπτιστήν	Σατανᾶν	Ἰούδαν
G.	προφήτου	βαπτιστοῦ	Σατανᾶ	Ἰούδα
D.	προφήτῃ	βαπτιστῇ	Σατανᾷ	Ἰούδᾳ

This rule (*NR.9*) requires us to place a circumflex accent on the penult of *προφῆτα*, rather than an acute (which would have been required had the final *α* been construed long). In oxytone words like *βαπτιστής*, there is no reason to change the accent from the acute accent, found in the nominative singular, to a circumflex, because *NR.1* and *NR.2* are rigorously applied.

In words declined like Σατανᾶς, *NR.3* clearly comes into play, and is in fact a subset of *NR.9*. In first declension words like Ἰούδας, the rule's exception comes into play: if the *a* is long in the nominative singular, it remains long throughout the inflectional variations.

Indeclinable Words

IWR.1 The accents on indeclinable words adhere to the General Rules, but must be learned by inspection.

Comment: Indeclinable words, precisely because they are indeclinable, do not offer the student the accentuation problems bound up with declensions and conjugations. On the other hand, they do not come under the recessive rule, or anything similar, to fix exactly the position and kind of accent they require. Therefore accents on indeclinable words must be learned by inspection. We have already come across several words in this category: ὦ, καί, Ἰσραήλ and (ἡ) Ἰερουσαλήμ.

The latter two are particularly interesting because they are examples of words transliterated (not translated) from Hebrew. As such, they are not proper Greek words; and therefore some editors do not accent them at all. Those who do accent them sometimes disagree where the accents should be placed! But these are special problems which affect only one small subset of indeclinable words.

Prepositions, adverbs and conjunctions are all indeclinable. Not a few prepositions, and a few adverbs, belong to a group of words which have no accent, called *proclitics*. These are discussed systematically in Lesson 9. Examples are included in the vocabulary for this lesson. Many adverbs are formed in one particular way which fixes their accents: these, too, will be discussed later (Lesson 25). At the moment, only one further rule affecting indeclinable words need be provided, and it concerns prepositions and conjunctions:

IWR.2 In elision, oxytone prepositions and conjunctions lose their accent.

Comment: ἀπό is an oxytone preposition. Because of *GR.6*, its acute accent is displaced by a grave accent when the word is immediately succeeded by another word: e.g., ἀπὸ αὐτοῦ. Nevertheless the preposition by itself is considered oxytone (the accent classification of a word is normally made when the word is in isolation); and therefore, according to this rule (*IWR.2*), when it is elided it loses its accent: e.g., ἀπ' αὐτοῦ. Similarly for the conjunction ἀλλά: ἀλλὰ ἔφη becomes ἀλλ' ἔφη. Note carefully, however, that *IWR.2* applies to words under two strict conditions: the words must be oxytone, and they must be prepositions or conjunctions.[1] In other words, *IWR.2* applies only to a subset of indeclinable words.

At the end of Lesson 5, I indicated one situation in which ἐστίν becomes ἔστιν, viz. when it stands at the head of its clause. Another may now be added: ἐστίν becomes ἔστιν when it is immediately preceded by the proclitic οὐκ: i.e., οὐκ ἔστιν. The formal rules surrounding ἔστιν in general and this change in particular must wait until Lesson 9.

The proper accentuation of the following vocabulary should be carefully memorized.

Nouns

βαπτιστής	προφήτης	Ἠλείας
ἐργάτης	στρατιώτης	Ἰούδας
Ἰωάννης (or Ἰωάνης)	τελώνης	νεανίας
κριτής	ὑποκριτής	Σατανᾶς
μαθητής	Ἀνδρέας	

Indeclinable Words

Unaccented
εἰς
ἐκ (ἐξ)
ἐν
οὐ (οὐκ, οὐχ)

Accented
ἀλλά
ἀπό
ἄρα (meaning 'therefore, then')
γάρ
δέ
οὐδέ
πρός

1. Oxytone words other than prepositions and conjunctions retain their accent, but on the preceding syllable: i.e., they become proparoxytone (counting the syllables as if no elision had taken place). For example, ἑπτά in elision becomes proparoxytone: i.e., ἑπτὰ ἦσαν becomes ἔπτ᾽ ἦσαν. But there are no examples of this in the New Testament, apart from doubtful variants.

Exercise

1. ὑποκριτα, τηρεις τας ἐντολας ἀλλ᾽ οὐ φιλεις τον θεον.
2. ὁ Παυλος μαρτυρει τῃ ἀληθειᾳ του εὐαγγελιου και τῃ σοφιᾳ του θεου.
3. οἱ ἐργαται βαλλουσιν λιθους εἰς την θαλασσαν;
4. λεγει οὐν ὁ Ἰησους, Ὁ υἱος του ἀνθρωπου ἐστιν ἐν ταις των οὐρανων νεφελων.
5. ἐστιν Ἰησους· σωζει γαρ τον λαον ἀφ᾽ ἁμαρτιας.
6. οἱ ἐργαται οὐχ εὑρισκουσιν την ὁδον εἰς τον σταυρον, και την θυσιαν του Ἰησου οὐ θεωρουσιν.
7. Ἰωαννης ἀρα γινωσκει τον ἀδελφον Ἰουδα.
8. οἱ στρατιωται βαλλουσιν Ἀνδρεαν τον ἀποστολον εἰς φυλακην.
9. ἐν τῃ ἡμερᾳ της δοξης βλεπομεν τον Χριστον προσωπον προς προσωπον.
10. ὁ οὐν κριτης οὐ λαμβανει το ἀργυριον ἀπο των πρεσβυτερων της ἐκκλησιας, οὐδε μισει τους ἀποστολους.

LESSON **8**

Second and First Declension Adjectives

Adjectives follow accent patterns similar in many respects to those of nouns. In fact we may form the first Adjective Rule in terms of the Noun Rules.

AR.1 Second and first declension adjectives adopt accent patterns like those laid down for nouns in *NR.1, NR.2, NR.4* and *NR.6.*

Comment: As applied to adjectives, *NR.1* will require that the student learn the accent of the adjective in the nominative singular *masculine* form: it is the nominative singular *masculine* form of the word which provides the base toward which all the other cases, genders and numbers seek to accommodate themselves, as nearly as the General Rules permit. *NR.2* can be applied without modification: 'In both the first and second declensions, when the ultima is accented at all, it has the circumflex accent in the genitives and datives of both numbers, and elsewhere the acute.' As applied to adjectives, *NR.4* stipulates that adjectives in the nominative or accusative neuter plural have a short ultima (i.e., a short α in the ultima): e.g., ἅγια (neuter plural, nominative or accusative), not ἁγία. As applied to adjectives, *NR.6* specifies that the α in the ultima of all accusative plural forms *of the feminine gender* of second declension adjectives, must always be considered long. Hence, in the adjective δίκαιος, the accusative plural of the feminine gender is δικαίας: the accent shifts to the penult because the ultima is considered long.

It is important to understand *AR.1* as a *limiting* rule: that is, it limits adjectives to following the patterns of *NR.1, NR.2, NR.4* and *NR.6.* It does not permit adjectives to copy other Noun Rules. For instance, second and first declension adjectives cannot follow *NR.3,* which lays down a rule for

nouns with a circumflex on the ultima, because a second declension noun
in the nominative masculine singular always has a short ultima and therefore cannot possibly be a perispomenon (δίκαιος, ἀγαθός, etc.). Again,
although first declension *nouns* suddenly shift their accent to a circumflex
on the ultima in the genitive plural (*NR.5*), *adjectives* do not do so—not
even adjectives in the feminine gender, where the closest parallel with first
declension feminine nouns is maintained. Similar comments could be made
about *NR.7*, *NR.8*, and *NR.9*.

Two examples will lay out the implications of *AR.1* for adjectives:

	M	F	N
Sing. **N.**	ἀγαθός	ἀγαθή	ἀγαθόν
V.	ἀγαθέ	ἀγαθή	ἀγαθόν
A.	ἀγαθόν	ἀγαθήν	ἀγαθόν
G.	ἀγαθοῦ	ἀγαθῆς	ἀγαθοῦ
D.	ἀγαθῷ	ἀγαθῇ	ἀγαθῷ
Plur. **N.V.**	ἀγαθοί	ἀγαθαί	ἀγαθά
A.	ἀγαθούς	ἀγαθάς	ἀγαθά
G.	ἀγαθῶν	ἀγαθῶν	ἀγαθῶν
D.	ἀγαθοῖς	ἀγαθαῖς	ἀγαθοῖς

	M	F	N
Sing. **N.**	ἔσχατος	ἐσχάτη	ἔσχατον
V.	ἔσχατε	ἐσχάτη	ἔσχατον
A.	ἔσχατον	ἐσχάτην	ἔσχατον
G.	ἐσχάτου	ἐσχάτης	ἐσχάτου
D.	ἐσχάτῳ	ἐσχάτη	ἐσχάτῳ
Plur. **N.V.**	ἔσχατοι	ἔσχαται	ἔσχατα
A.	ἐσχάτους	ἐσχάτας	ἔσχατα
G.	ἐσχάτων	ἐσχάτων	ἐσχάτων
D.	ἐσχάτοις	ἐσχάταις	ἐσχάτοις

Both of the above examples are words whose stems end in a consonant
other than ρ. It will be remembered that second declension adjectives whose
stems end in a vowel or ρ follow a different paradigm in the feminine
singular, viz. α instead of η suffixes. Because α is ambiguous, we must again
spell out whether it is long or short:

AR.2 Second declension adjectives with stems ending in a vowel or ρ (and
which therefore have an α suffix in the feminine singular of all cases)
construe the α in the ultima of all feminine singular forms as long.

Chapter 8

Comment: Obviously, this will not affect the accent of every adjective with a stem ending in a vowel or ρ; but it will affect such words if they are proparoxytones or properispomena. A good example might be δίκαιος:

	M	F	N
Sing. N.	δίκαιος	δικαία	δίκαιον
V.	δίκαιε	δικαία	δίκαιον
A.	δίκαιον	δικαίαν	δίκαιον
G.	δικαίου	δικαίας	δικαίου
D.	δικαίῳ	δικαίᾳ	δικαίῳ
Plur. N.V.	δίκαιοι	δίκαιαι	δίκαια
A.	δικαίους	δικαίας	δίκαια
G.	δικαίων	δικαίων	δικαίων
D.	δικαίοις	δικαίαις	δικαίοις

Similar patterns will be followed by, *inter alia*, ὅμοιος, ἅγιος, and other such proparoxytones. Note carefully that the only thing which distinguishes the nominative-vocative feminine singular form from the nominative-accusative neuter plural form is the accent: δικαία and δίκαια respectively. Observe, too, that *AR.2*, for adjectives, provides an accent pattern for proparoxytones in the feminine singular cases, quite different from that provided by *NR.7* and *NR.8* for proparoxytone nouns. Contrast:

Sing. N.V.	ἀλήθεια	δικαία
A.	ἀλήθειαν	δικαίαν
G.	ἀληθείας	δικαίας
D.	ἀληθείᾳ	δικαίᾳ

Here, then, are some properly accented second and first declension adjectives with stems ending in a consonant other than ρ, and three compound adjectives. (The next lesson will provide accented vocabulary made up largely of second and first declension adjectives with stems ending in a vowel or ρ.)

ἀγαθός	καλός	πτωχός
ἀγαπητός	λοιπός	σοφός
δυνατός	μέσος	τυφλός
ἕκαστος	μόνος	
ἔσχατος	ὀλίγος	ἄπιστος
ἱκανός	πιστός	ἀκάθαρτος
καινός	πρῶτος	αἰώνιος
κακός	τρίτος	

Exercise

1. ἐν ταις ἐσχαταις ἡμεραις ὀλιγοι ἐχουσιν την ἀγαπην.
2. οἱ κακοι προφηται οὐ μαρτυρουσιν τῃ ἀληθειᾳ.
3. ὁ ἀποστολος ὁ ἀγαπητος πρωτον γραφει καινην ἐπιστολην τῃ ἐκκλησιᾳ.
4. ὁ Ἀνδρεας πρωτος μαθητης του Χριστου ἐστιν.
5. μονος Παυλος μενει πιστος;
6. ὁ Ἰησους θεραπευει τους τυφλους και τους λεπρους.
7. οἱ φιλοι ἐχουσιν ἱκανον ἀργυριον.
8. τα λοιπα παιδια αἰτει ἀρτον ἀπο των ἀδελφων του Ἰησου.
9. ὁ θεος κρινει ἑκαστον νεανιαν.
10. οἱ σοφοι οὐ γινωσκουσιν τον θεον τῃ σοφιᾳ, ἀλλ᾽ οἱ πτωχοι ζητουσιν την βασιλειαν του θεου.

Enclitics and Proclitics

Preliminary Definitions

1. A *proclitic* is a word which normally has no accent, because it is read so closely with the following word as to 'lean' (cf. προκλίνω, 'to lean forward') upon it.

The following are the proclitics found in the New Testament: the definite article in the forms ὁ, ἡ, οἱ and αἱ; the conjunctions εἰ and ὡς; the prepositions εἰς, ἐκ (or ἐξ), ἐν; and the negative οὐ (or οὐκ, οὐχ).

2. An *enclitic* is a word which, whenever possible, is read so closely with the preceding word that it has no accent of its own (cf. ἐγκλίνω, 'to lean upon').

The following are the enclitics found in the New Testament: the pronouns μέ, μοῦ, μοί; σέ, σοῦ, σοί; the indefinite pronoun τὶς in all its declensional forms; the indefinite adverbs πού, ποτέ, πώ and πώς; the particles γέ and τέ; all the present indicative forms of εἰμί *except* the second person singular εἶ: i.e., εἰμί, ἐστίν, ἐσμέν, ἐστέ, εἰσίν; and similarly the present indicative forms of φημί, *except* the second person singular φῇς: but only φημί, φησίν and φασίν are found in the New Testament.

The enclitics are printed here with the accent each must have when it is in a situation where it has to have its *own* accent: at other times some of these enclitics must take on an accent other than what is normally their own. (The rules follow, *infra*.) The grave accent on the indefinite pronoun indicates it never has an accent of its own: when it is accented, it is because of some other word nearby, and never because the pronoun itself is being stressed. This is quite unlike other enclitics.

Clearly, since accentuation is reckoned from the end of words, enclitics are far more significant than proclitics, as far as accents are concerned. Nevertheless the following rules affect both enclitics and proclitics to some degree, and we may label them Enclitic/Proclitic Rules.

EPR.1 The word before an enclitic does not change an acute accent on the ultima to a grave accent.

Comment: Clearly, this refers to oxytones; and it is in contravention of *GR.6*. Hence, ἀδελφός is correct, and so is ὁ ἀδελφὸς ὁ ἀγαθός; but if ἀδελφός were succeeded by an enclitic, the correct accentuation would be ὁ ἀδελφός μου. *EPR.1* is not followed, however, when for some reason the enclitic retains its accent. Hence, although πρός σε is correct, yet if for some reason (e.g., *EPR.6.1, infra*) the σε is accented, then the correct accentuation would be πρὸς σέ.

EPR.2 If the word preceding an enclitic has an acute accent on the ante-penult, or a circumflex accent on the penult, then there is an additional accent, an acute, on the ultima.

Comment: Hence, δοῦλός μου; ἄνθρωπός μου, ὅτι δέ ἐστε υἱοί (Gal. 4:6); οὗτός ἐστιν ὁ ἄνθρωπος (Acts 21:28); φωνεῖτέ με (John 13:13); ἡ γλῶσσά μου (Acts 2:26).

EPR.3 If the word preceding an enclitic has an acute accent on the penult, then:

EPR.3.1 a disyllabic enclitic retains its accent;
EPR.3.2 a monosyllabic enclitic loses its accent.

Comment: Hence, ὁ λόγος μου; but ὁ λόγος ἐστὶν ἀγαθός. It should be noticed that enclitics which consist of long syllables are, for purposes of accent, treated as if they were short when they are added to a preceding word. For this reason ὁ λόγος μου is not anomalous.

EPR.4 If the word preceding an enclitic has a circumflex accent on the ultima, then both monosyllabic and disyllabic enclitics normally lose their accent.

Comment: This rule is the result of modern philological research into the Greek of the first century. Older grammars (including their reprints!) say rather that if the word preceding an enclitic has a circumflex accent on the ultima, then a disyllabic enclitic *retains* its accent, even though a monosyllabic enclitic *loses* its accent (compare *EPR.3.1* and *EPR.3.2, supra*). Such a formulation is admittedly more consistent, and it certainly reflects the intonation of Attic Greek. Hence Westcott and Hort, who largely follow Attic practice, have not only ὁ ὀπίσω μου (John 1:15), but μετ᾽ αὐτῶν ἐστιν ὁ νυμφίος (Matt. 9:15), ὑμῖν εἰμί (I Cor. 9:2), and *αὐτῶν ἐστὶν ἡ βασιλεία* (Matt. 5:3). Nevertheless, for the period of Greek reflected in the New Testament, it is certainly correct to follow *EPR.4*. Hence, the United Bible Societies *Greek New Testament*, and the Nestle/Aland text, are to be followed when, although they accept *ὁ ὀπίσω μου* (John 1:15), they insist on *μετ᾽ αὐτῶν ἐστιν ὁ νυμφίος* (Matt. 9:15), *ὑμῖν εἰμι* (I Cor. 9:2), and *αὐτῶν ἐστιν ἡ βασιλεία* (Matt. 5:3).

EPR.5 If the word before an enclitic is itself a proclitic (except *οὐ, οὐκ, οὐχ*) or an enclitic, it has an acute accent on the ultima.

Comment: Hence, *μάρτυς γάρ μού ἐστιν ὁ θεός* (Rom. 1:9), and *τῶν χειρῶν σού εἰσιν οἱ οὐρανοί* (Heb. 1:10). Both these examples are important for another reason: they illustrate the fact that *μου* and *σου*, under the influence of this rule, can take an accent other than the one they might be expected to take (when they are accented at all), viz. the circumflex, *μοῦ* and *σοῦ*. *EPR.5* is a powerful rule. Indeed, if a series of enclitics follows one after another, then each enclitic throws an acute accent back on the preceding one: e.g., *εἴ τίς τί σοί φησιν*. The enclitics *μου* and *σου, even though succeeded by an enclitic*, may take the circumflex that is their own accent, rather than the acute accent, if *μου* or *σου* is being emphasized: contrast *σύνδουλός σού εἰμι* (Rev. 19:10) and *δέδωκάς μοι παρὰ σοῦ εἰσιν* (John 17:7). Similarly, this entire rule (*EPR.5*) may be overridden if the enclitic before which a proclitic or another enclitic appears, is itself emphatic, because then it will itself be accented (cf. *EPR.6.1, infra*), vitiating the need for the previous enclitic or proclitic to gain an accent.

Note, too, that according to *EPR.5*, an enclitic can throw an accent back onto a proclitic as easily as onto an enclitic. This produces anomalous patterns such as *εἴς με* and the like.

It is important to notice that *EPR.5* is concerned only with an *enclitic* preceded by an enclitic or a proclitic. If a *proclitic* is preceded by an enclitic, no special information is necessary since the enclitic will be related to *its* preceding word, not to the proclitic. If a proclitic is preceded by another proclitic, neither proclitic is accented: e.g., *οὐχ ὡς ἐγὼ θέλω* (Matt. 26:39).

EPR.6 An enclitic retains its accent when:

> **EPR.6.1** there is emphasis on the enclitic;
> **EPR.6.2** the enclitic stands at the head of its clause;
> **EPR.6.3** the enclitic is preceded by *οὐ, οὐκ*, or *οὐχ*, as a separate word.

Comment: In short, the difference between ἐγώ εἰμι and ἐγὼ εἰμί is the slight difference between 'I am' and 'I *am*'. It is often difficult to be certain whether an enclitic in the New Testament should be accented or not, since accents were not included in the original uncial scripts. But editorial decisions have to be made, just as they have to be made for punctuation. About many examples there can really be very little doubt: e.g., ἵνα τέκνα θεοῦ κληθῶμεν· καὶ ἐσμέν (I John 3:1—'in order that we should be called sons of God; *and such we are*'). Some examples are perhaps more doubtful: e.g., Mark 9:17, ἤνεγκα τὸν υἱόν μου πρὸς σέ. Note, however, that if the enclitic retains its accent, as σέ does in this clause, then the preceding word does *not* follow the enclitic rules which normally pertain (in this instance *EPR.1*). An example of an enclitic accented because it is located at the head of its clause is found in John 13:13: εἰμὶ γάρ. Modern editors of the Greek New Testament also adopt *EPR.6.3*: e.g., ὅτι ἡμεῖς οὐκ ἐσμὲν ἀδόκιμοι (II Cor. 13:6), not ὅτι ἡμεῖς οὐκ ἐσμεν ἀδόκιμοι; or again, οἱ γὰρ ἄρχοντες οὐκ εἰσὶν φόβος (Rom. 13:3), not οἱ γὰρ ἄρχοντες οὐκ εἰσιν φόβος. The only exception is οὐκ preceding ἐστίν: this must be treated separately (*EPR.8.3, infra*). The phrase "as a separate word" rules out of consideration compound words such as οὔτε: see *EPR.9, infra*.

EPR.7 When a proclitic stands alone or at the end of a clause, it is then accented.

Comment: This is particularly applicable to the negative particle: e.g., ὁ δὲ φησιν, οὔ (Matt. 13:29). Note that *EPR.7* applies only to proclitics, not to enclitics.

EPR.8 The verbal form ἐστίν becomes ἔστιν, completely losing its character as an enclitic:

EPR.8.1 when it stands at the beginning of a sentence or clause;
EPR.8.2 when signifying existence or possibility;
EPR.8.3 when it is preceded by οὐκ, μή, ὡς, εἰ, καί, ἀλλά (or ἀλλ'), τοῦτο (when elided as τοῦτ');
EPR.8.4 when it is strongly emphatic.

Comment: It is most important to observe that this rule applies to ἐστίν alone, not to the entire present indicative of εἰμί. Thus, ἐστίν, like any other disyllabic enclitic, is mildly emphatic in its own right when it retains its accent on the ultima. But the paroxytone form, ἔστιν, is unique, and must not be stretched to other enclitics. Examples of ἔστιν under *EPR.8.1* are found in John 21:25, I Cor. 15:44. τὸ μνῆμα αὐτοῦ ἔστιν ἐν ὑμῖν (Acts 2:29) is an example of ἔστιν signifying existence (*EPR.8.2*): cf. also Acts 19:2. *EPR.8.3* is self-explanatory, and there are many examples: e.g., οὐκ ἔστιν (Gal. 3:12), τοῦτ' ἔστιν (Rom. 7:18). It should be noted, however, that of the seven words listed in *EPR.8.3*, ὡς+ἐστίν does not occur in the New Testament, and when τοῦτο is not elided then the rule is not applied (e.g., τοῦτό ἐστιν, John 6:29). Rev. 17:18 is very emphatic (*EPR.8.4*).

EPR.9 When an enclitic forms the last part of a compound word, the compound is accented as if the enclitic were a separate word.

Comment: If it appears that General Rules are violated in words such as οὔτε, ὥσπερ and ὥστε, it must be remembered that originally each of these words was a combination of separate proclitic and enclitic: e.g., ὡς+τέ. *EPR.5* then requires ὥς τε; and it is but a short step to ὥστε.

Enclitics and proclitics will be presented in several vocabulary lists in future lessons. For the moment we may restrict ourselves to the present indicative of the verb to be, all of whose conjugational forms are enclitic except the second:

> εἰμί
> εἶ (not an enclitic)
> ἐστίν
> ἐσμέν
> ἐστέ
> εἰσίν

The rules for accenting enclitics and proclitics are so inter-related that it seems best to study them together, even though, for the moment, the student must learn to apply the Enclitic/Proclitic Rules to the above forms only, not neglecting the intricacies of the anomalous ἐστίν.

Additional properly accented second declension adjectives, this time with stems ending in a vowel or ρ, are also provided:

ἅγιος	ἕτερος	νέος
ἄξιος	ἴδιος	ὅμοιος
δεξιός	ἰσχυρός	παλαιός
δεύτερος	καθαρός	πλούσιος
δίκαιος	μακάριος	πονηρός
ἐλεύθερος	μικρός	

Exercise

1. μακαριοι εἰσιν οἱ καθαροι ἐν τῃ καρδιᾳ.
2. ὁ παλαιος οἰνος ἐστιν ἀγαθος, ὁ δε νεος ἐστιν κακος.
3. οἱ ἁγιοι βλεπουσιν την δοξαν των οὐρανων και μαρτυρουσιν ταις φωναις των ἀγγελων.
4. ὠ ὑποκριτα, εἰ ὁ δουλος νεκρων ἐργων.
5. ὁ υἱος του ἀνθρωπου ἐχει τριτον πειρασμον ἐν τῃ ἐρημῳ.
6. ἐστε ἐχθροι του σταυρου του Χριστου.
7. ἡ προσευχη του Φαρισαιου οὐκ ἐστιν καθαρα.
8. οἱ πλουσιοι οὐκ εἰσιν ἐλευθεροι ἀπο της ἐξουσιας του θεου.
9. ὁ θεος ἐγειρει τον Ἰησουν ἐκ των νεκρων.
10. οἱ ἐχθροι Χριστου εἰσιν τεκνα του διαβολου.

The Imperfect Indicative Active; Compound Verbs

The Imperfect Indicative Active

The basic verb rule (*VR.1*) is followed throughout the imperfect indicative: e.g.,

$$\ \ \ \ \ \ \check{\epsilon}\lambda υον$$
$$\ \ \ \ \ \ \check{\epsilon}\lambda υες$$
$$\ \ \ \ \ \ \check{\epsilon}\lambda υεν$$
$$\ \ \ \ \ \ \dot{\epsilon}\lambda \acute{υ}ομεν$$
$$\ \ \ \ \ \ \dot{\epsilon}\lambda \acute{υ}ετε$$
$$\ \ \ \ \ \ \check{\epsilon}\lambda υον$$

Similarly, the rule for accenting contract verbs (*VR.2*, including *VR.2.1* and *VR.2.2*) fixes the accent for contract verbs in the imperfect:

ἐφίλε+ον	→ ἐφίλουν
ἐφίλε+ες	→ ἐφίλεις
ἐφίλε+ε	→ ἐφίλει
ἐφιλέ+ομεν	→ ἐφιλοῦμεν
ἐφιλέ+ετε	→ ἐφιλεῖτε
ἐφίλε+ον	→ ἐφίλουν

Although it is possible to figure this out from first principles for every -εω verb, it is worth noting that the pattern of accents in the imperfect active of φιλέω will duplicate itself in the imperfect active of all -εω verbs:

viz., an acute accent on the last syllable of the stem of the singular forms and of the third person plural, and a circumflex accent on the contracted syllable of the first and second persons plural. For instance:

ἤτουν	ἐθεώρουν	μετενόουν
ἤτεις	ἐθεώρεις	μετενόεις
ἤτει	ἐθεώρει	μετενόει
ἠτοῦμεν	ἐθεωροῦμεν	μετενοοῦμεν
ἠτεῖτε	ἐθεωρεῖτε	μετενοεῖτε
ἤτουν	ἐθεώρουν	μετενόουν

The basic recessive rule (*VR.1*) is no less applicable in an irregular imperfect like that of ἔχω:

$$εἶχον$$
$$εἶχες$$
$$εἶχεν$$
$$εἴχομεν$$
$$εἴχετε$$
$$εἶχον$$

Compound Verbs

VR.3 In compound verbs, the accent cannot go farther back than the augment.

Comment: Thus, in ἀπῆγον (the imperfect of ἀπάγω), in defiance of the recessive rule the accent cannot go farther back than the η: hence, ἀπῆγον (the General Rules specify what kind of accent, once *VR.3* has specified where it must go). This rule holds wherever there is a compound verb in a tense which requires an augment; but for the moment we shall restrict ourselves to compound verbs in the imperfect.

All the verbs are, of course, accented according to the basic verb rule (*VR.1*), and so do not suffer from the ambiguity of the basic noun rule. Therefore they do not need to be listed here with correct accent, since the accent is automatically fixed: hence ἄγω, φέρω, etc.

Exercise

1. *ὁ Ἰησους παρελαμβανεν μικρα παιδια, και τα μικρα παιδια ἠκουεν του Ἰησου.*
2. *αἱ παρθενοι ὑπηγον ἐκ του οἰκου.*
3. *ὁ δε Χριστος φερει σταυρον και περισσευει ἐν ἀγαπῃ.*
4. *ἐχαιρομεν ἐν Κυριῳ, ἠγεν γαρ την ἐκκλησιαν εἰς την ἀληθειαν.*
5. *οἱ προφηται ἐδιδασκον τα τεκνα ἐν τῃ ἐρημῳ.*
6. *ὁ Ἰησους ἠνοιγεν τους ὀφθαλμους των τυφλων, και ἐπεγινωσκεν τους ἰδιους φιλους.*
7. *προσεφερομεν το ἀργυριον τῳ τελωνῃ, ἀλλ᾽ ἐδιωκεν τους πλουσιους και τους πτωχους.*
8. *οἱ ἐχθροι του λαου ἀπεθνησκον ἐν φυλακῃ, ὁ δε κριτης ἀπελυεν ὀλιγους δουλους.*
9. *Ἰωαννης ὁ βαπτιστης οὐκ ἐποιει σημεια.*
10. *οὐκ ἐδιδασκεν τα τεκνα, οὐδε ἀπηγεν την ἰδιαν γενεαν ἀπο των ὁδων της ἀδικιας.*

Demonstratives; αὐτός, ἑαυτόν, and ἀλλήλους; Imperfect of εἰμί

Demonstratives and Other Pronouns

For purposes of accentuation, most pronouns follow the accent patterns of second declension adjectives. In fact, this may be laid down as a rule for pronouns:

PR.1 Unless otherwise specified, pronouns follow the accent patterns laid down for adjectives in *AR.1*.

Comment: The words 'unless otherwise specified' should be noted: examples of exceptions to *PR.1* will come later, especially in Lessons 14 and 22. To give detailed examples of the sweep of *PR.1*, several pronouns are fully declined below, with correct accentuation. In each instance it is necessary to learn the location of the accent in the nominative singular masculine; the accents for all the declensional forms of that word are then fixed by *PR.1*. It is essential that the student work out for himself, on the basis of *PR.1*, exactly why each declensional form has the accent it does. This will enable him not only to accent the forms correctly from first principles, but will ultimately make the accenting of such common words second nature.

Some of the pronouns below function on occasion as adjectives (e.g., the demonstratives ἐκεῖνος and οὗτος, and the personal pronoun αὐτός, which can serve as an identical adjective); but we shall classify them simply as pronouns following *PR.1*. In any event, *PR.1* itself establishes that there is no essential difference between the patterns of accents of these pronouns and those regulated by the basic rule for adjectives.

		M	F	N
Sing.	N.	ἐκεῖνος	ἐκείνη	ἐκεῖνο
	A.	ἐκεῖνον	ἐκείνην	ἐκεῖνο
	G.	ἐκείνου	ἐκείνης	ἐκείνου
	D.	ἐκείνῳ	ἐνείνη	ἐκείνῳ
Plur.	N.	ἐκεῖνοι	ἐκεῖναι	ἐκεῖνα
	A.	ἐκείνους	ἐκείνας	ἐκεῖνα
	G.	ἐκείνων	ἐκείνων	ἐκείνων
	D.	ἐκείνοις	ἐκείναις	ἐκείνοις
Sing.	N.	οὗτος	αὕτη	τοῦτο
	A.	τοῦτον	ταύτην	τοῦτο
	G.	τούτου	ταύτης	τούτου
	D.	τούτῳ	ταύτῃ	τούτῳ
Plur.	N.	οὗτοι	αὗται	ταῦτα
	A.	τούτους	ταύτας	ταῦτα
	G.	τούτων	τούτων	τούτων
	D.	τούτοις	ταύταις	τούτοις
Sing.	N.	αὐτός	αὐτή	αὐτό
	A.	αὐτόν	αὐτήν	αὐτό
	G.	αὐτοῦ	αὐτῆς	αὐτοῦ
	D.	αὐτῷ	αὐτῇ	αὐτῷ
Plur.	N.	αὐτοί	αὐταί	αὐτά
	A.	αὐτούς	αυτάς	αὐτά
	G.	αὐτῶν	αὐτῶν	αὐτῶν
	D.	αὐτοῖς	αὐταῖς	αὐτοῖς
Sing.	A.	ἑαυτόν	ἑαυτήν	ἑαυτό
	G.	ἑαυτοῦ	ἑαυτῆς	ἑαυτοῦ
	D.	ἑαυτῷ	ἑαυτῇ	ἑαυτῷ
Plur.	A.	ἑαυτούς	ἑαυτάς	ἑαυτά
	G.	ἑαυτῶν	ἑαυτῶν	ἑαυτῶν
	D.	ἑαυτοῖς	ἑαυταῖς	ἑαυτοῖς

Plur.	A.	ἀλλήλους
	G.	ἀλλήλων
	D.	ἀλλήλοις

In studying these forms, note with special care such small differences as those between αὕτη and αὐτή, and whence such differences derive.

To these words we may add the adjectives ὅλος and ἄλλος, both of which decline regularly (like ἀγαθός) and follow the adjective rules. The word ἄλλος is especially to be noted, because in the neuter plural nominative, ἄλλα, it is distinguishable from the indeclinable ἀλλά only by the accent.

Imperfect of εἰμί

This follows the normal verb recessive rule:

> ἤμην
> ἦς or ἦσθα
> ἦν
> ἦμεν or ἤμεθα
> ἦτε
> ἦσαν

Note, however, that the forms ἦς and ἦν could in theory have been ἧς and ἥν respectively: no verb rule precludes this possibility. Similarly, one could not guess by inspection (apart from the accent) whether the final α in ἦσθα was short or long: had it been the latter, the word would have been paroxytone, ἤσθα. The correct accentuation, however, has been provided; and where there is ambiguity because the verb rules are not sufficiently specific, this correct accentuation must be learned.

Exercise A

1. ἐκεινα δε τα δενδρα ἐβαλλον εἰς την θαλασσαν.
2. οὗτοι οἱ πρεσβυτεροι δοκουσιν τυφλοι.
3. αὗται ἐμενον ἐν τω πλοιω.
4. οὗτος οὖν ὁ δευτερος ἀδελφος διηκονει και προσεκυνει τω θεω ἐν ἑτερω ἱερω.
5. παρεκαλουμεν και ἐφωνουμεν, ἀλλ᾽ οὐκ ἠκολουθουν.
6. οἱ πτωχοι ἐγαμουν και κατῳκουν ἐν τη γη.
7. ὅλη γαρ ἡ συναγωγη ἐδοκει ὁμοια προβατοις.
8. ἡ ἀγαπη και ἡ ἀληθεια εἰσιν ἐν τη αἰωνιω βασιλεια του θεου.
9. ἐν τη ὡρα ἐκεινη ἐχαιρομεν.
10. ἐκεινος ὁ πονηρος διακονος ἐδει τον ἰδιον υἱον.

Exercise B

1. αὕτη ἐστιν ἡ ἀγαπη του θεου.
2. αἱ λοιπαι της κωμης συνηγον τα προβατα αὐτων ἐν μεσῳ του ἀγρου.
3. οἱ αὐτοι μαθηται ηὐχαριστουν τῳ πλουσιῳ τελωνῃ.
4. ἐκεινοι ἠσαν ἑτεροι ἀρτοι και ἀλλο ποτηριον.
5. ἡς ὑποκριτης και ἠμεθα τυφλοι.
6. αὐτοι παρελαμβανομεν αὐτους εἰς το ἑτερον πλοιον.
7. ἀλλο παιδιον βαλλει ἑαυτο εἰς την θαλασσαν.
8. οἱ αὐτοι Ἰουδαιοι οὑτοι ἠκουον και ἠκολουθουν τοις ἰδιοις προφηταις.
9. ἠμην ἀγαπητος, ἀλλ᾿ ἐμισειτε ἀλληλους.
10. ἐβλεπετε τους υἱους αὐτης ἐν τῃ ἐκκλησιᾳ.

More Indeclinable Words; Present and Imperfect Indicative Passive

The purpose of this lesson is not to introduce new accent rules but to apply some of the rules already learned to new words and new inflections.

More Indeclinable Words

Review *IWR.1* and *IWR.2*, Lesson 7. The following words are all either prepositions or adverbs which sometimes function as prepositions; and of course they are indeclinable. Their accents should be noted.

διά, δι᾽	κατά, κατ᾽, καθ᾽	πρό
ἔμπροσθεν	μετά, μετ᾽, μεθ᾽	σύν
ἐνώπιον	ὀπίσω	ὑπέρ
ἔξω	παρά, παρ᾽	ὑπό, ὑπ᾽, ὑφ᾽
ἐπί, ἐπ᾽, ἐφ᾽	περί	χωρίς

To these must be added two further indeclinable words, which sometimes function as conjunctions and sometimes as prepositions:

ἄχρι
ἕως

Present and Imperfect Indicative Passive

Review the verb rules, *VR.1*, *VR.2* and *VR.3*, Lessons 3, 4 and 10.

The present and imperfect indicative passive (and middle), being finite parts of the verb, follow the basic recessive rule; and therefore their accents are completely fixed. For example:

λύομαι	ἐλυόμην
λύῃ	ἐλύου
λύεται	ἐλύετο
λυόμεθα	ἐλυόμεθα
λύεσθε	ἐλύεσθε
λύονται	ἐλύοντο

Similarly, *VR.2*, which applies to contract verbs, when rigorously applied to -εω verbs in these tenses and voices, completely fixes the accent:

φιλέ+ομαι	→ φιλοῦμαι	ἐφιλε+όμην	→ ἐφιλούμην
φιλέ+ῃ	→ φιλῇ	ἐφιλέ+ου	→ ἐφιλοῦ
φιλέ+εται	→ φιλεῖται	ἐφιλέ+ετο	→ ἐφιλεῖτο
φιλε+όμεθα	→ φιλούμεθα	ἐφιλε+όμεθα	→ ἐφιλούμεθα
φιλέ+εσθε	→ φιλεῖσθε	ἐφιλέ+εσθε	→ ἐφιλεῖσθε
φιλέ+ονται	→ φιλοῦνται	ἐφιλέ+οντο	→ ἐφιλοῦντο

Once again it is worth pointing out that, although the accent can be figured out from first principles for every form, yet the *pattern* of accents will remain constant for each of the two conjugations, regardless of the -εω verb being accented.

Exercise A

1. ὁ διδασκαλος ἐστιν ὑπερ τον μαθητην.
2. πτωχοι ἠσαν ἐν τῳ Ἰσραηλ ἐπι Ἡλειου του προφητου.
3. οὐκ ἐστε ὑπο νομον, ἀλλ᾽ ὑπο την ἀγαπην.
4. ἐν τριτῃ ἡμερᾳ ἐζητουν σημειον παρ᾽ αὐτου ἐκ του οὐρανου.
5. ὑπηγον κατ᾽ ἰδιαν εἰς τας ἰδιας οἰκιας.
6. ὁ θεος ἐστιν ὑπερ του λαου αὐτου, ἀλλ᾽ οἱ ἐργαται Σατανα εἰσιν κατα της ἐκκλησιας.
7. δι᾽ ἀνθρωπου ἐστιν ὁ θανατος, ἀλλ᾽ ὁ Χριστος τηρει τους ἰδιους μαθητας ἑως της παρουσιας αὐτου.
8. ἡ της σωτηριας χαρα περισσευει χωρις του νομου.
9. προ ἐκεινης της ὡρας οὐκ ἐθεωρουν την δοξαν αὐτου οὐδε ἠκουον την φωνην αὐτου.
10. ἡ αὐτη χηρα περιπατει περι την κωμην.

Exercise B

1. οὗτοι οἱ λογοι ἐλαλουντο ὑπο των ἀποστολων ἐνωπιον των πρεσβυτερων.
2. ἐπεμπεσθε μετα των προφητων ἐμπροσθεν του ὀχλου.
3. το μνημειον ᾠκοδομειτο ὑπο το ἱερον.
4. ἦγες τον λαον ὀπισω του ἀγαπητου προφητου δια της ἐρημου εἰς τα Ἱεροσολυμα.
5. οἱ φιλοι ἐπεμπον ὀλιγους ἀρτους προς ἀλληλους, και ὀλιγον οἰνον και ἱκανον ἀργυριον προς τους ἀξιους ἀδελφους τους ἐν φυλακῃ.
6. μετ᾽ ἐκεινας τας ἡμερας οἱ λοιποι στρατιωται ὑπηγον ἐξω της κωμης.
7. ὦ ὑποκριτα, οὐ λαλεις περι των ἐντολων του Κυριου.
8. μετ᾽ οὖν ταυτα ἐλαλουμεν τον λογον του θεου τοις μαθηταις.
9. ἐκλαιετε ὑπερ ἀπιστων και των ἀκαθαρτων.
10. αὐτοι οἱ νεανιαι ἐδιδασκοντο ὑπο των ἰδιων διδασκαλων.

The Relative Pronoun;
The Present Imperative;
More Indeclinable Words

The Relative Pronoun

The relative pronoun follows the basic pronoun rule (*PR.1*). This means that it is accented exactly like the article, except for the four forms of the article which are proclitics (viz. *ὁ*, *ἡ*, *οἱ*, *αἱ*). The fully declined relative pronoun is accented as follows:

	M	F	N
Sing. N.	ὅς	ἥ	ὅ
A.	ὅν	ἥν	ὅ
G.	οὗ	ἧς	οὗ
D.	ᾧ	ᾗ	ᾧ
Plur. N.	οἵ	αἵ	ἅ
A.	οὕς	ἅς	ἅ
G.	ὧν	ὧν	ὧν
D.	οἷς	αἷς	οἷς

If accents are not used, it is impossible to distinguish the relative pronoun *ἥ* from the article *ἡ*; the relative pronoun (neuter nominative or accusative) *ὅ* from the article (masculine nominative) *ὁ*; and the relative pronouns *οἵ* and *αἵ* from the corresponding articles *οἱ* and *αἱ*. Of course, because relative pronouns are only rarely followed by punctuation, they will normally be found with a *grave* or a circumflex accent, instead of an *acute* or a circumflex accent.[1] The corresponding forms of the article, however, normally take *no* accent; so it is usually easy to distinguish between articles and relative pronouns even when the spelling and breathing of the one might be confused with the other.

The exception occurs when a normally proclitic article does take an accent. This takes place when the succeeding word is an enclitic (cf. *EPR.5*): e.g., contrast ὅ ἐστιν μεθερμηνευόμενον Χριστός (John 1:41), and ὅ τε Πέτρος (Acts 1:13). The context of the two expressions eliminates the possible ambiguity, and shows that the ὅ in John 1:41 is the relative pronoun, whereas the ὅ in Acts 1:13 is the article.

The following sample sentences should be studied closely.

1. βλέπω τοὺς πρεσβυτέρους οἳ ἀκολουθοῦσιν.
2. οἱ δοῦλοι οὓς πέμπετε φωνοῦσιν.
3. αὕτη ἐστὶν ἡ γραφὴ ἣ τηρεῖται ἐν τῇ συναγωγῇ.
4. αὕτη ἐστὶν ἡ γραφὴ ἣν εἶχεν ὁ ἀπόστολος.
5. τὰ παιδία ἃ ἐδίδασκον κλαίει.
6. ὁ προφήτης οὗ ἀναγινώσκεις τὰ βιβλία ἅγιός ἐστιν.
7. οἱ νεανίαι οἷς ποιῶ τοῦτο δοῦλοί εἰσιν.
8. ὃς οὐ λαμβάνει τὸν σταυρὸν αὐτοῦ, οὐκ ἔστιν ἄξιος.

The Present Imperative

The present imperative follows the basic verb rule (*VR.1*), and therefore takes a recessive accent:

Active	Middle/Passive
λῦε	λύου
λυέτω	λυέσθω
λύετε	λύεσθε
λυέτωσαν	λυέσθωσαν

Note that the υ in the stem is considered long: this is made clear in the form λῦε.

By following *VR.2*, regarding contract verbs, we arrive at the following accents:

1. This is why some grammars accent relative pronouns as ἥ, ὅ, οἵ, and αἵ. Formally however, the accentuation of any word is established when the word stands independently, not when it occurs in flow. The proper accentuation therefore is ἥ, ὅ, οἵ and αἵ, even though the grave forms are the ones normally found in the New Testament.

Active		Passive	
φίλε+ε	→ φίλει	φιλέ+ου	→ φιλοῦ
φιλε+έτω	→ φιλείτω	φιλε+έσθω	→ φιλείσθω
φιλέ+ετε	→ φιλεῖτε	φιλέ+εσθε	→ φιλεῖσθε
φιλε+έτωσαν	→ φιλείτωσαν	φιλε+έσθωσαν	→ φιλείσθωσαν

Although it is possible to figure out the correct accentuation for each -εω verb in the imperative mood, once again it may be easier to memorize the pattern of accents, since that pattern will be repeated for all -εω verbs.

More Indeclinable Words

Verbs in the imperative mood are normally negated by μή, not οὐ. The latter is a proclitic; the former an oxytone. To this we may also add the oxytone διό, which derives from δι ' ὅ.

The particles οὐ and μή are used not only to negate things, but also to ask questions which expect certain responses. When they function in the latter capacity, they may take on the lengthened forms οὐχί and μητί: note that *both* of these words are oxytones.

All of the accents in the following sentences are either possible or required:

> ἔστιν ὁ Χριστός;
> μὴ ἔστιν ὁ Χριστός;
> μήτι ἐστὶν ὁ Χριστός;
> οὐκ ἔστιν ὁ Χριστός;
> οὐχί ἐστιν ὁ Χριστός;

Both οὐ and μή may combine with δέ from οὐδέ and μηδέ respectively. Again, both οὐ and μή may combine with the enclitic τε to form οὔτε and μήτε respectively. Neither of the accents on these two words is anomalous: οὔτε (not οὔτε) and μήτε (not μῆτε) are correct, because these words were originally conceived as οὔ τε and μή τε respectively. (See *EPR.5* and the discussion in Lesson 9.)

Exercise

1. λαμβανε το ποτηριον και χαιρε ἐν τουτῳ τῳ δευτερῳ σημειῳ της δικαιοσυνης, της εἰρηνης και της ζωης.
2. λυου ἀπο της ἁμαρτιας καθ᾽ ἡμεραν.
3. ἡ ἀρχη της ἐξουσιας ἐστιν ἡ δοκει ὁμοια νεῳ οἰνῳ.

4. οὐχὶ ἡ πρωτη ἦν ἐσχατη;
5. ὁ διδασκαλος ὅς ἐστιν ἀξιος τῆς τιμης πιστευετω τῳ βιβλιῳ και προσ-
   κυνειτω τῳ θεῳ.
6. μητι ἐκαλει κακους εἰς τον φοβον του θεου;
7. ἀνοιγετε ἐκαστην θυραν, τουτο γαρ ἐστιν δυνατον παρα τῳ θεῳ.
8. την δικαιοσυνην ἐνδυετε την καρδιαν και θυσιαι προσφερεσθωσαν ἐν
   μεσῳ του ναου.
9. οἱ νεκροι μη εἰσιν μακαριοι;
10. αἱ παρθενοι αἱ ἠσθιον τον ἀρτον οὐκ ἐκρινον ἑαυτας.

LESSON **14**

First and Second Person Personal Pronouns, Possessive Adjectives, and Reflexive Pronouns; More Indeclinable Words

First and Second Person Personal Pronouns

Review the pronoun rule, *PR.1*, Lesson 10: 'Unless otherwise specified, pronouns follow the accent patterns laid down in *AR.1*.' We now come to pronominal forms which fall under the 'otherwise specified' rubric. The first and second person personal pronouns can be set forth in an array which brings out the anomalies:

		First Person		**Second Person**	
		Follows PR.1	**Enclitic**	**Follows PR.1**	**Enclitic**
Sing.	*N.*	ἐγώ		σύ	
	A.	ἐμέ	μέ		σέ
	G.	ἐμοῦ	μοῦ		σοῦ
	D.	ἐμοί	μοί		σοί
Plur.	*N.*	ἡμεῖς		ὑμεῖς	
	A.	ἡμᾶς		ὑμᾶς	
	G.	ἡμῶν		ὑμῶν	
	D.	ἡμῖν		ὑμῖν	

The plural forms are perispomenon throughout. The *a* in the ultima of the accusative plural, ἡμᾶς and ὑμᾶς, is, like the *a* in the accusative plural of first declension nouns, clearly construed as long.

67

But the singular forms are not so simple. Outside the nominative (i.e., the so-called *oblique* cases), the first person personal pronoun has two forms: one which follows *PR.1*, and the other a set of enclitics. Among the second person personal pronouns, in the singular number and oblique cases, only the enclitic form exists.

The accent placed on these enclitic forms shows what is normal when the accent is retained; but precisely because the words are enclitics, the accents are not normally retained. Recall, too, that an enclitic whose accent (when it is retained) is a circumflex (e.g., μοῦ, σοῦ), can on occasion take the acute accent instead: review Lesson 9.

Normally the longer forms of the first person singular ἐμέ, ἐμοῦ and ἐμοί are used for emphasis or with most prepositions. The enclitic forms are more common, and are more likely to be found with the adverb/prepositions ἐνώπιον, ἔμπροσθεν and ὀπίσω, and with the preposition πρός.

First and Second Person Possessive Adjectives

Like other second declension adjectives, first and second person possessive adjectives follow *AR.1* exactly. Hence:

		First Person			Second Person		
		M	F	N	M	F	N
Sing.	N.	ἐμός	ἐμή	ἐμόν	σός	σή	σόν
	A.	ἐμόν	ἐμήν	ἐμόν	σόν	σήν	σόν
	G.	ἐμοῦ	ἐμῆς	ἐμοῦ	σοῦ	σῆς	σοῦ
	D.	ἐμῷ	ἐμῇ	ἐμῷ	σῷ	σῇ	σῷ
Plur.	N.	ἐμοί	ἐμαί	ἐμά	σοί	σαί	σά
	A.	ἐμούς	ἐμάς	ἐμά	σούς	σάς	σά
	G.	ἐμῶν	ἐμῶν	ἐμῶν	σῶν	σῶν	σῶν
	D.	ἐμοῖς	ἐμαῖς	ἐμοῖς	σοῖς	σαῖς	σοῖς

Some of these forms are not found in the New Testament; but clearly those that are found decline like ἀγαθός, -ή, -όν and are accented according to *AR.1*.

First and Second Person Reflexive Pronouns

In the singular, first and second person reflexive pronouns are made up of ἐμέ and σέ combined with the appropriate declensional forms of αὐτός, and are accented like αὐτός.

First Person		Second Person	
M	**F**	**M**	**F**
ἐμαυτόν	ἐμαυτήν	σεαυτόν	σεαυτήν
ἐμαυτοῦ	ἐμαυτῆς	σεαυτοῦ	σεαυτῆς
ἐμαυτῷ	ἐμαυτῇ	σεαυτῷ	σεαυτῇ

In the plural, of course, the first and second person reflexive pronouns utilize the third person plural reflexive pronoun forms (cf. Lesson 10), and need not be repeated here.

The pronoun ἐγώ provides a common example of *crasis*, discussed in Lesson 1: καὶ ἐγώ may appear as κἀγώ. The first of the combining words loses its accent. Similarly, καὶ ἐκεῖνος is more elegantly written as κἀκεῖνος.

More Indeclinable Words

> μέν
> ὡς (a proclitic)
> καθώς
> ὥσπερ[1]
> ὥστε[1]

Exercise

1. ἐμοι μεν ἐδοκει σοφον, οἱ δε ἠκολουθουν ἑτερᾳ ὁδῳ.
2. κρατειτε ἐμε, λαε Ἰουδαιας, και σωζετε ἑαυτους ἐκ ταυτης της πονηρας γενεας.
3. διηκονουν σοι και ἐδουν ἑαυτους τῃ αἰωνιῳ διαθηκῃ σου.
4. κἀγω προσφερω θυσιας, ἁς παραλαμβανει ὁ θεος.
5. κἀγω εἰμι ἐν μεσῳ ὑμων ὡς διακονος.
6. τουτο δε ἐστιν το σημειον της σης παρουσιας.
7. οὐκ εἰμι ὡσπερ οἱ λοιποι των ἀνθρωπων.
8. ὁ δε λεγει ἡμιν, Προσφερετε τους πτωχους προς με.
9. συ περι σεαυτου μαρτυρεις· ἡ μαρτυρια σου ἐστιν ἀκαθαρτος.
10. ὁ διδασκαλος ὁς οὐκ ἐστιν μετ᾽ ἐμου κατ᾽ ἐμου ἐστιν.

---

1. These words are not sporting anomalous accents because they were originally formed from the proclitic ὡς and the enclitics περ and τε respectively: cf. *EPR.9.*

The Present Infinitive; δύναμαι; The Future Active

The Present Infinitive

VR.4 The present infinitive in all voices has a recessive accent.

Comment: The reason it is necessary to specify that the present infinitive has a recessive accent is that *VR.1* assigns a recessive accent *only to the finite parts of a verb*. The fact that the present infinitives also have a recessive accent is coincidental: other infinitives, we shall later see, are not so helpful.

The present infinitives are thus λύειν and λύεσθαι. In contract verbs, *VR.2* prevails:

$$\varphi\iota\lambda\acute{\varepsilon}+\varepsilon\iota\nu \rightarrow \varphi\iota\lambda\varepsilon\tilde{\iota}\nu$$
$$\varphi\iota\lambda\acute{\varepsilon}+\varepsilon\sigma\theta\alpha\iota \rightarrow \varphi\iota\lambda\varepsilon\tilde{\iota}\sigma\theta\alpha\iota$$

All -εω contracts will have a circumflex accent on the contracted syllable of present infinitives.

The present infinitive of εἰμί is εἶναι. This is not an enclitic.

The Verb δύναμαι

Although δύναμαι is highly irregular in its inflections, its accents follow *VR.1* rigorously.

Pres. Indic.	Imperf. Indic.	Pres. Inf.
δύναμαι	ἐδυνάμην	δύνασθαι
δύνασαι	ἐδύνασο	
δύναται	ἐδύνατο	
δυνάμεθα	ἐδυνάμεθα	
δύνασθε	ἐδύνασθε	
δύνανται	ἐδύναντο	

The Future Active

The future active follows *VR.1*, and therefore the accent is completely specified. Here are three examples:

λύσω	γράψω	ἕξω
λύσεις	γράψεις	ἕξεις
λύσει	γράψει	ἕξει
λύσομεν	γράψομεν	ἕξομεν
λύσετε	γράψετε	ἕξετε
λύσουσιν	γράψουσιν	ἕξουσιν

The so-called contract verbs do not contract outside the present and imperfect tenses; and so they are accented according to *VR.1* without reference to *VR.2*.

φιλήσω	καλέσω
φιλήσεις	καλέσεις
φιλήσει	καλέσει
φιλήσομεν	καλέσομεν
φιλήσετε	καλέσετε
φιλήσουσιν	καλέσουσιν

Two verbs used in the following exercises are the impersonal δεῖ (imperf. ἔδει, from the contract δέω), and the impersonal ἔξεστιν, which is *not* an enclitic. Obviously these adhere to the basic verb rule *VR.1*, and need not be discussed.

Exercise A

1. μη ἔξεστιν αὐτοις λαμβανειν το ἀργυριον ἀπο των τελωνων;
2. αἱ νεφελαι ὑπαγουσιν και αἱ ψυχαι των ἀνθρωπων θελουσιν εὐχαριστειν.

3. ἠθελομεν οὖν θεραπευειν τους υἱους αὐτων.
4. και δια το περισσευειν την ἀδικιαν ἡ ἀγαπη ἀποθνησκει;
5. ἐδει τον Ἰησουν ἀπαγειν τους μαθητας ἀπο της Γαλιλαιας.
6. οἱ δε ὀχλοι ἐχαιρον ἐν τῳ αὐτους ἀκουειν και βλεπειν τα σημεια ἁ ἐποιει.
7. ὁ ἀνεμος ἠν ἰσχυρος ὡστε βαλλειν το πλοιον ἐπι τας πετρας.
8. μητι δυναμεθα ποιειν τουτο;
9. ἐν δε τῳ συναγεσθαι τους πρεσβυτερους ἐμενομεν ἐν τοις ἀγροις.
10. οὐ μισω τον ἐχθρον μου ὡστε με δυνασθαι τον θεον φιλειν.

Exercise B

1. ἀνοιξω τα βιβλια ἁ ἐστιν ἐν τη συναγωγη.
2. πεμψω προς αὐτους σοφους και προφητας, ἀλλ᾽ οὐκ ἀκουσουσιν αὐτων οἱ υἱοι Ἰσραηλ.
3. οἱ λεπροι ἐξουσιν τα προβατα ἁ σωζεται ἀπο των ἀνεμων και της θαλασσης.
4. πεισομεν ἀρα τους ἰδιους ἀδελφους ἐκβαλλειν τους δεξιους ὀφθαλμους αὐτων;
5. και καλεσουσιν το τεκνον Ἰησουν, σωζει γαρ τον λαον αὐτου ἀπο των ἁμαρτιων αὐτων.
6. ἐν δε τῳ τον ὀχλον ἀκουειν τον λογον τα δαιμονια ἠγεν θυσιας του προσφερειν αὐτας τῳ Σατανᾳ.
7. ἠσθενει δε το δενδρον δια το μη ἐχειν γην.
8. οὐχι ἐστιν ὁ καιρος του πιστευειν;
9. θεωρησομεν το προσωπον του Κυριου ἐν τῳ ἱερῳ ὁ οἰκοδομειται ἐν τοις Ἱεροσολυμοις.
10. διο φωνει ἡμιν καθ᾽ ἡμεραν προς το παρακαλειν ἡμας.

The Verbal Stem;
The Middle Voice;
The Future of εἰμί

The Verbal Stem

The move from the present stem to verbal stem leaves the basic verb rule, *VR.1*, untouched. In other words, the recessive rule still operates, and definitely fixes the accent in all the finite forms. For example, the present indicative active βαπτίζω has the verbal stem βαπτιδ and therefore the future βαπτίσω; but the recessive rule operates on each form as it stands, and determines the accentuation.

The Middle Voice

In form, the present and imperfect middle are exactly like the present and imperfect passive, and so no new problems of accentuation arise. This is true not only of the indicative mood, but also of the imperative and infinitive.

The future middle (but not the future passive) is formed from the present middle in exactly the same way that the future active is formed from the present active; and the same recessive rule still applies. Hence:

$$\text{λύσομαι}$$
$$\text{λύσῃ}$$
$$\text{λύσεται}$$
$$\text{λυσόμεθα}$$
$$\text{λύσεσθε}$$
$$\text{λύσονται}$$

This rule, *VR.1*, is applicable even when highly irregular stems occur. Hence, the future of the deponent middle verb ἔρχομαι is ἐλεύσομαι; the future of γίνομαι is γενήσομαι; and the future of δύναμαι is δυνήσομαι. But in none of these instances is *VR.1* contravened.

The Future of εἰμί

The verb εἰμί conjugates in the future as follows:

> ἔσομαι
> ἔσῃ
> ἔσται
> ἐσόμεθα
> ἔσεσθε
> ἔσονται

None of these forms is an enclitic (unlike the present tense), and all of them adhere to *VR.1*.

Exercise A

1. καθαριζετε τας ἰδιας καρδιας και περιπατησετε ἐνωπιον μου ἐν ὁδοις της χαρας.
2. κηρυσσετε τας ἐπαγγελιας και φυλασσετε τας ἐντολας ἐν τῳ ὑμας ἑτοιμαζειν την ὁδον της δοξης.
3. ὁ δε πτωχος κραξει ἐν μεσῳ του ἱερου.
4. πρασσετε την δικαιοσυνην ἀλληλοις και δοξασετε τον μονον θεον.
5. και ἀποκαλυψω την ἁμαρτιαν των ἀνθρωπων οἱ πρασσουσιν την ἀδικιαν, και κρυψουσιν τους ὀφθαλμους αὐτων ἀπ᾽ ἐμου.
6. ἀπηρχοντο γαρ προς την ἐρημον ἐν ᾗ αὐτος ὁ Ἰωαννης ἐβαπτιζεν.
7. κἀκεινος δεχεται τους ἁμαρτωλους οἱ ἐρχονται προς αὐτον και ἐσθιει μετ᾽ αὐτων.
8. δει ὑμας ἀποκρινεσθαι ταυτη τη γενεᾳ.
9. αὐτος ὁ Χριστος ἀρξει της ἐκκλησιας, και ὁ λαος αὐτου προσευξεται και εὐαγγελισεται.
10. ὁ δε οὐκ ἠθελεν πορευεσθαι ἐν ταις ὁδοις της ἀληθειας.

The First Aorist Active;
The Second Aorist Active

The First Aorist Active

The finite parts of the first aorist active follow the basic verb rule, *VR.1*. Hence:

Indicative	Imperative
ἔλυσα	λῦσον
ἔλυσας	λυσάτω
ἔλυσεν	λύσατε
ἐλύσαμεν	λυσάτωσαν
ἐλύσατε	
ἔλυσαν	

This paradigm illustrates an important rule:

VR.5 Whenever a is found in the ultima of first aorist active forms or of perfect active forms, it is always short.

Comment: If this were not so, then, for instance, ἔλυσα would have to give way to ἐλύσα. As stated, the rule applies to perfect active forms as much as to aorist active forms: we will make use of this information in Lesson 26.

Note that the υ in the imperatival form λῦσον is long. This is not so for all verbs, and must be learned by inspection.

From these paradigms and from *VR.5*, one may derive ἐδίωξα, ἔγραψα, ἔπεισα, ἔκρυψα, ἐφίλησα, and so forth.

75

The infinitive is λῦσαι. Not being part of the finite verb, *VR.1* does not apply. In fact, another rule is necessary:

VR.6 The first aorist infinitive active is accented on the penult.

Comment: On a two syllable word like λῦσαι, one might be forgiven for thinking, wrongly, that the aorist infinitive follows the recessive rule. A quick examination of longer infinitives, however, shows this is *not* so: e.g., ἑτοιμάσαι is clearly not recessive. Moreover, when the vowel in the penult could be construed as long or short (e.g., when the vowel is υ, α, or ι), the distinction must be learned by inspection. Hence, κρῦψαι is correct; but so is ἑτοιμάσαι.

The Second Aorist Active

The second aorist indicative follows the recessive rule. For example:

ἔβαλον	ἥμαρτον	ἔπεσον
ἔβαλες	ἥμαρτες	ἔπεσες
ἔβαλεν	ἥμαρτεν	ἔπεσεν
ἐβάλομεν	ἡμάρτομεν	ἐπέσομεν
ἐβάλετε	ἡμάρτετε	ἐπέσετε
ἔβαλον	ἥμαρτον	ἔπεσον

The second aorist imperative, too, normally follows the recessive rule; but there are several qualifications which forbid a sweeping generalization. When *VR.1* is followed, verbs will conjugate and be accented as follows:

βάλε
βαλέτω
βάλετε
βαλέτωσαν

However, the following points must be observed:

1. The Attic dialect had a tendency to accent several second aorist imperative second person singular verbs as oxytones, clearly breaking *VR.1*: in particular, εἰπέ, ἐλθέ, εὑρέ, ἰδέ and λαβέ. The first three appear as oxytones in κοινή Greek as well; and some editors accept other entries.

2. The most recent editors of the Greek New Testament tend to preserve the recessive rule in *almost* all forms (e.g., παράλαβε, Matt. 2:13; βάλε, Matt. 4:6).

3. The exceptions are the verbs εἰπέ (related to λέγω) and ἐλθέ (related to ἔρχομαι). When these two imperatives, in the second person singular

only, enjoy the normal second aorist inflections, they become oxytones. However, these two verbs are also examples of second aorists which sometimes appear with first aorist endings: *ἤλθατε* instead of *ἤλθετε* (Matt. 25:36), *εἶπαν* instead of *εἶπον* (Luke 11:2), and the like. When this phenomenon afflicts the second person singular of the (normally) second aorist imperative, then *εἰπέ* becomes *εἶπον* (by influence from *λῦσον*), and *ἐλθέ* becomes *ἔλθον*; or, alternatively, some editors prefer to accent these words too as oxytones (i.e., *εἰπόν* and *ἐλθόν*). See, for example, from the third edition of the UBS Greek New Testament, *εἰπόν* (Acts 28:26). Observe, too, that although *ἐλθέ* is oxytone (e.g., Matt. 14:29), nevertheless compounds of this imperatival form adhere to the recessive rule: e.g., *εἴσελθε* (Acts 9:6).

In order to gain some measure of order, it is recommended that the student adopt the following rule:

VR.7 For purposes of order, all second aorist active imperatives should be made to follow *VR.1* (the recessive rule), *except* the second person singular of the second aorist imperative of the forms corresponding to *λέγω* and *ἔρχομαι* (but not their compounds). This exception holds true regardless of whether such forms are pure second aorist or mixed second and first aorist.

Comment: This rule is not really satisfactory, but it reveals the current state of the discussion. Framing *VR.7* in this way does not quite *require* that the irregular forms be accented as oxytones, but pretty much expects it.

VR.8 The second aorist active infinitive has a circumflex accent on the ultima.

Comment: Thus, *βαλεῖν* is distinguished from *βάλλειν* both by stem and by accent.

Note the accents on the following irregular second aorists of *γινώσκω* and *-βαίνω* (the preparatory hyphen indicates the word is found only in compounds: e.g., *ἀποβαίνω, καταβαίνω*):

ἔγνων	-ἔβην
ἔγνως	-ἔβης
ἔγνω	-ἔβη
ἔγνωμεν	-ἔβημεν
ἔγνωτε	-ἔβητε
ἔγνωσαν	-ἔβησαν

The basic verb rule *VR.1* has been followed throughout.

The first three principal parts of a number of verbs are provided below, with correct accentuation. The student should be able to explain each accent mark.

Present	Future	Aorist
ἄγω	ἄξω	ἤγαγον
		(Inf. ἀγαγεῖν)
-βαίνω	-βήσομαι	-έβην
γινώσκω	γνώσομαι	ἔγνων
ἔρχομαι	ἐλεύσομαι	ἦλθον
		(Inf. ἐλθεῖν)
ἐσθίω	φάγομαι	ἔφαγον
εὑρίσκω	εὑρήσω	εὗρον
ἔχω	ἕξω	ἔσχον
(Imperf. εἶχον)		
λαμβάνω	λήμψομαι	ἔλαβον
ὁράω	ὄψομαι	εἶδον
		(Inf. ἰδεῖν)
πίνω	πίομαι	ἔπιον
φέρω	οἴσω	ἤνεγκον
		(Inf. ἐνεγκεῖν)

Other verbs will be included in the exercises; but the principles of accentuation remain constant for each form introduced.

Two more common New Testament words and their accents should be noted at this point: ἴδε and ἰδού. Because the first of these words, formally speaking, is the aorist imperative active second person singular of εἶδον, the accent is specified by the recessive rule. The second word, ἰδού, is, formally speaking, the aorist imperative middle second person singular of εἶδον; and this, as we shall see in Lesson 19, normally has a circumflex accent on the ultima (e.g., γενοῦ). But both ἴδε and ἰδού have by New Testament times become interjections rather than parts of the finite verb; and one word is now accepted as paroxytone, the other as oxytone.

Exercise A

1. οὐδὲ ἐδίωξαν τοὺς τελώνας οἱ ἀπῆγον τα προβατα.
2. ἐπεμψας γαρ τας χηρας ἀγορασαι τα ἱματια.
3. διηρχεσθε την καλην γην ἑτοιμασαι τον ἐλευθερον λαον.
4. ἐργατα ἰσχυρε, κρυψον τους λιθους οἱ περισσευουσιν ἐν τω ἀγρω.
5. καθαρισατε και ἁγιασατε τας καρδιας ὑμων.

6. βουλονται δε ἀδικησαι την τιμην των λοιπων;
7. ἡ γαρ φωνη του Ἰωαννου ἐκραξεν ἐν τῃ ἐρημῳ, Ἑτοιμασατε την ὁδον τῳ Κυριῳ.
8. και ἐτηρησαμεν τας ἐντολας ἁς ἠκουσαμεν ἀπο των πιστων στρατιωτων.
9. καλον ἐστιν αὐτους τα αὐτα ἀναγινωσκειν.
10. μετα ταυτα την ἐξουσιαν μου και τας χρειας μου ἀποκαλυψω αὐτοις.

Exercise B

1. ἀνεβημεν εἰς το ἱερον ἐν ἐκεινῃ τῃ ὡρᾳ.
2. ὠ Κυριε, ἡμαρτον ἐνωπιον σου.
3. οἱ δε προφηται ἐφυγον εἰς την ἐρημον.
4. οὑτος ἐστιν ὁ λιθος ὁς ἐπεσεν ἐκ του οὐρανου.
5. εὑρον δε το ἀργυριον και αὐτο ἠγαγον αὐτοις ὡστε αὐτους παραλαβειν τον μισθον αὐτων.
6. οἰσει δε τον σταυρον και πιεται το ποτηριον.
7. ἐμαθον γαρ παθειν και ὀψονται το προσωπον αὐτου.
8. εἰδομεν δε τον ἡλιον και εἰπομεν λογους της χαρας και της μετανοιας.
9. λημψομεθα την δυνατην σωτηριαν αὐτου και γνωσομεθα την εἰρηνην αὐτου.
10. και ἐν τῳ ἀγαγειν αὐτους το παιδιον του προσενεγκειν αὐτο τῳ Κυριῳ, ὁ λαος ηὐλογησεν τον θεον.

Liquid Verbs;
More Indeclinable Words

Liquid Verbs

VR.9 In the future tense, active or middle voice, liquid verbs have the same accents as do -εω verbs in the present tense, active or middle voice.

Comment: Hence, the futures of ἐγείρω and πίπτω are, respectively:

ἐγερῶ	πεσοῦμαι
ἐγερεῖς	πεσῇ
ἐγερεῖ	πεσεῖται
ἐγεροῦμεν	πεσούμεθα
ἐγερεῖτε	πεσεῖσθε
ἐγεροῦσιν	πεσοῦνται

To discover the factors which generate these accents is to discover that the accents are not as anomalous as they might at first appear. In the development of the language there was at one time a σ expected of these futures; but this σ was shielded from the labial of the stem by an ε designed to facilitate pronunciation: hence, ἐγειρέσω, ἐγειρέσεις, and so on. In time the σ dropped out: ἐγειρέ(σ)ω → ἐγειρέω, which is formally just like the present indicative active of (uncontracted) φιλέω (note the characteristic ου and ει diphthongs in first and second person plural forms). The result is ἐγειρῶ. However, such shifting of the accent toward the end of the word can easily produce subtle changes in the stem, usually some kind of shortening of vowel sounds. The result is ἐγερῶ.[1] Similar explanations stand behind all liquid stem futures.

---

1. For further discussion of the changes in spelling which accentuation can effect, cf. Lesson 37, *infra*.

Liquid verbs whose stems are the same for both the present tense and
the future tense (e.g., *μένω* and *κρίνω*) distinguish present from future by
accent alone, except in the first and second plural forms where the short
penult of the present gives way to the long penult of the future. For
example:

μένω	*μενῶ*
μένεις	*μενεῖς*
μένει	*μενεῖ*
μένομεν	*μενοῦμεν*
μένετε	*μενεῖτε*
μένουσιν	*μενοῦσιν*

The first (or second) aorist of liquid verbs offers no particular problem
of accentuation, but follows the normal recessive rule. For example:

ἀπέστειλα
ἀπέστειλας
ἀπέστειλεν
ἀπεστείλαμεν
ἀπεστείλατε
ἀπέστειλαν

Similarly, the aorist imperative of this verb is *ἀπόστειλον* (recessive accent),
and the aorist infinitive *ἀποστεῖλαι* (*VR.6*).

The first three principal parts of a number of liquid verbs are provided
below, with correct accentuation. The student should be able to explain
each accent mark. Dashes indicate that the expected form does not occur in
the New Testament, and so it has been eliminated from the list.

Present	Future	Aorist
ἀγγέλλω	*ἀγγελῶ*	*ἤγγειλα*
αἴρω	*ἀρῶ*	*ἦρα*
ἀποθνήσκω	*ἀποθανοῦμαι*	*ἀπέθανον*
ἀποκτείνω	*ἀποκτενῶ*	*ἀπέκτεινα*
ἀποστέλλω	*ἀποστελῶ*	*ἀπέστειλα*
βάλλω	*βαλῶ*	*ἔβαλον*
ἐγείρω	*ἐγερῶ*	*ἤγειρα*
κρίνω	*κρινῶ*	*ἔκρινα*
λέγω[2]	*ἐρῶ*	*εἶπον*
ὀφείλω	—	—
πίπτω	*πεσοῦμαι*	*ἔπεσον*

2. Clearly, *λέγω* is not a liquid verb; but its future has a liquid stem, and so the verb is
included here.

More Indeclinable Words

Two more should now be noted: ὅτι and ὅτε.

Exercise

1. *ὑμεις οὐ πιστευετε, ὅτι οὐκ ἐστε ἐκ των προβατων των ἐμων.*
2. *οὗτοι κρινουσιν* (future) *τας χηρας και ἀποκτενουσιν* (future) *τα τεκνα αὐτων;*
3. *ἐμεινα δε ἐν τῳ ἰδιῳ τοπῳ ἑως ἀνεγνω το βιβλιον.*
4. *ὁ δε Ἰησους εἰπεν τῳ παραλυτικῳ, Ἀρον αὐτο και ὑπαγε εἰς τον οἰκον σου· ὅτε δε ἠκουσεν ταυτα ἠρεν αὐτο και ὑπηγεν.*
5. *εἰπον οὐν ὑμιν ὅτι ἀποθανεισθε ἐν ταις ἁμαρτιαις ἡμων.*
6. *και ἐρουσιν ὅτι Ἀπεθανεν ἐν τῃ πρωτῃ ἡμερᾳ ἑως ἠργαζομεθα.*
7. *ὑμεις λεγετε ὅτι βλασφημεις, ὅτι εἰπον, Υἱος του θεου εἰμι.*
8. *δυνασθε πιειν το ποτηριον ὁ δει με πιειν;*
9. *ἀλλ᾽ οἱ Φαρισαιοι ἐλεγον ὅτι ἐσθιει παρα ἁμαρτωλῳ.*
10. *παρηγγειλατε αὐτοις μη ἀδικησαι ὁλον τον λαον.*

First and Second Aorist Middle

The first aorist middle follows the basic verb rule (*VR.1*) in both the indicative and the imperative. The infinitive is accented on the antepenult, and therefore is recessive in its own right (contrast the first aorist infinitive *active*, *VR.6*).

Indicative	Imperative	Infinitive
ἐλυσάμην	λῦσαι	λύσασθαι
ἐλύσω	λυσάσθω	
ἐλύσατο	λύσασθε	
ἐλυσάμεθα	λυσάσθωσαν	
ἐλύσασθε		
ἐλύσαντο		

The second aorist middle, used by few verbs in the New Testament but rendered common because γίνομαι requires it, calls for an additional rule.

VR.10 The second aorist imperative middle second person singular has a circumflex accent on the ultima; and the second aorist infinitive middle has an accent on the penult.

Hence:

Indicative	Imperative	Infinitive
ἐγενόμην	γενοῦ	γενέσθαι
ἐγένου	γενέσθω	
ἐγένετο	γένεσθε	
ἐγενόμεθα	γενέσθωσαν	
ἐγένεσθε		
ἐγένοντο		

Comment: Obviously, in terms of accent one must carefully distinguish between γίνεσθαι and γενέσθαι, and between γίνου and γενοῦ.

Exercise

1. ὑμεις μεν ἠρνησασθε τον ἁγιον και δικαιον κατ' ἰδιαν, ὁ δε ἠρνησατο αὐτον ἐμπροσθεν ὁλου του λαου.
2. αὐτον δει τον οὐρανον δεξασθαι, ἀλλ' ὀψομεθα αὐτον ἐν τῃ ἡμερᾳ της δευτερας παρουσιας αὐτου.
3. Πετρε, ἐλθε εἰς την οἰκιαν της ἀπιστου και ἀσπασαι αὐτην.
4. μη γινεσθε ὁμοιοι τοις ὑποκριταις, ἀλλα γινεσθε πιστοι ἀλληλοις.
5. ὁ δε πρωτος παρεγενετο και εἰπεν, Κυριε, βουλομεθα μαθειν προσευξασθαι.
6. οὐκ ἐξεστιν προφητῃ ἀπολεσθαι ἐξω των Ἱεροσολυμων.
7. κἀκεινος ἀπωλετο, ἀλλ' οἱ υἱοι αὐτου οὐκ ἀπωλοντο.
8. και ἐγενετο ἐν τῳ σπειρειν ἀλλα ἐπεσεν παρα την ὁδον.
9. ἐν τῳ κοσμῳ ἠν, και ὁ κοσμος δι' αὐτου ἐγενετο, και ὁ κοσμος αὐτον οὐκ ἐγνω.
10. ἠρξω ἀπο των ἐσχατων ἑως των πρωτων.

LESSON **20**

Third Declension Masculine and Feminine Nouns with Consonant Stems

Third declension nouns normally follow *NR.1*, and therefore seek to preserve the accent on the same syllable as that on which the accent occurs in the nominative singular. However, because third declension inflections so often add a syllable to the end of the word, it must be made clear that by 'the same syllable' we mean the same syllable as counted from the *beginning* of the word. For example:

Sing. N.	ὁ ἀστήρ	ἡ ἐλπίς	
A.	ἀστέρα	ἐλπίδα	
G.	ἀστέρος	ἐλπίδος	
D.	ἀστέρι	ἐλπίδι	
Plur. N.	ἀστέρες	ἐλπίδες	
A.	ἀστέρας	ἐλπίδας	
G.	ἀστέρων	ἐλπίδων	
D.	ἀστράσιν	ἐλπίσιν	

Thus, although ἐλπίς is oxytone and ἐλπίδα paroxytone, nevertheless both forms have the accent on the second syllable, counting from the beginning of the word.

NR.10 Whenever an *a* occurs in the final syllable of accusative singular or accusative plural forms of third declension nouns, that *a* is short.

Comment: This is quite different from the first declension, where, for instance, the accusative plural (in -ας) is always considered long, and where complex rules govern other final syllables with *a* vowels (cf. *NR.4*,

85

NR.6, *NR.7*, *NR.8*, and *NR.9*). Knowledge of *NR.10* makes the accenting of nouns such as the following much easier than would otherwise be the case:

Sing.	*N.*	ὁ σωτήρ	ὁ ἄρχων	ὁ Ἕλλην	ὁ αἰών
	A.	σωτῆρα	ἄρχοντα	Ἕλληνα	αἰῶνα
	G.	σωτῆρος	ἄρχοντος	Ἕλληνος	αἰῶνος
	D.	σωτῆρι	ἄρχοντι	Ἕλληνι	αἰῶνι
Plur.	*N.*	σωτῆρες	ἄρχοντες	Ἕλληνες	αἰῶνες
	A.	σωτῆρας	ἄρχοντας	Ἕλληνας	αἰῶνας
	G.	σωτήρων	ἀρχόντων	Ἑλλήνων	αἰώνων
	A.	σωτῆρσιν	ἄρχουσιν	Ἕλλησιν	αἰῶσιν

NR.11 Monosyllabic nouns of the third declension normally accent the ultima in the genitive and dative of both numbers. In the genitive plural, that accent must be circumflex; elsewhere, acute.

Comment: The expression 'monosyllabic nouns' refers to nouns in the nominative singular, since normally monosyllabic nouns of the third declension in the oblique cases are not possible: the oblique cases *add a syllable*. Hence:

Sing.	*N.*	ἡ σάρξ	ἡ χείρ	ἡ νύξ
	A.	σάρκα	χεῖρα	νύκτα
	G.	σαρκός	χειρός	νυκτός
	D.	σαρκί	χειρί	νυκτί
Plur.	*N.*	σάρκες	χεῖρες	νύκτες
	A.	σάρκας	χεῖρας	νύκτας
	G.	σαρκῶν	χειρῶν	νυκτῶν
	D.	σαρξίν	χερσίν	νυξίν

Occasionally the same phenomenon occurs in third declension nouns of two syllables; but this is usually explainable. Consider the Greek word for 'dog':

Sing.	*N.*	ὁ κύων
	A.	κύνα
	G.	κυνός
	D.	κυνί
Plur.	*N.*	κύνες
	A.	κύνας
	G.	κυνῶν
	D.	κυσίν

The stem of κύων is irregular. Normally, third declension nouns form their oblique cases by adding a syllable; but here the nominative singular has the same number of syllables as the oblique forms. When this occurs, the accentuation acts as if the nominative singular had one less syllable—i.e., as if the nominative singular were monosyllabic. We see the same problem in the word δύο, whose dative plural is δυσίν (see Lesson 24, *infra*).

More problematic are the explicit exceptions to *NR.11*. These must be learned by inspection. Fortunately, they are quite rare and offer no problem. Consider the accent on the genitive plural in the following:

Sing. **N.**	ὁ or ἡ παῖς
A.	παῖδα
G.	παιδός
D.	παιδί
Plur. **N.**	παῖδες
A.	παῖδας
G.	παίδων
D.	παισίν

NR.12 Third declension nouns whose stems end in -αντ, and whose dative plural therefore has a penult which could be long or short, will always reckon that syllable long if it has an accent.

Comment: Consider the following noun:

Sing. **N.**	ὁ ἱμάς
A.	ἱμάντα
G.	ἱμάντος
D.	ἱμάντι
Plur. **N.**	ἱμάντες
A.	ἱμάντας
G.	ἱμάντων
D.	ἱμᾶσιν

This word has a circumflex in the penult of the dative plural, ἱμᾶσιν; and the accent is not expected, apart from the rule. It is important to note that there is no rule to apply to words like Ἕλλην or αἰών (fully declined above), because in the former word the accent is on the antepenult of the dative plural, and in both instances the vowel in the penult is *necessarily* long. Similarly, there is no need for a rule akin to *NR.12* to apply to the following nouns, because the first one enjoys a diphthong in the penult of the dative plural (and therefore the penult *must* be long), and in the second the vowel in the penult ensures that the penult *must* be short:

Sing.	N.	ὁ ὀδούς	ὁ ἡγεμών
	A.	ὀδόντα	ἡγεμόνα
	G.	ὀδόντος	ἡγεμόνος
	D.	ὀδόντι	ἡγεμόνι
Plur.	N.	ὀδόντες	ἡγεμόνες
	A.	ὀδόντας	ἡγεμόνας
	G.	ὀδόντων	ἡγεμόνων
	D.	ὀδοῦσιν	ἡγεμόσιν

In other words, *NR.12* removes an ambiguity connected with the trouble-some *a* in *-αντ* stems, and nothing more. Stems in *-εντ* and *-οντ* do not generate a similar ambiguity, because their dative plurals are normally *-εισιν* and *-ουσιν* respectively: the penult of each is necessarily long.

With the above rules in mind, the following nouns can be accented throughout their declensional forms without difficulty.

αἰών, αἰῶνος, ὁ; common in the expressions εἰς τὸν αἰῶνα and εἰς τοὺς
    αἰῶνας τῶν αἰώνων
ἀμπελών, ἀμπελῶνος, ὁ
ἄρχων, ἄρχοντος, ὁ
ἀστήρ, ἀστέρος, ὁ; dative plural ἀστράσιν
εἰκών, εἰκόνος, ἡ
Ἕλλην, Ἕλληνος, ὁ
ἐλπίς, ἐλπίδος, ἡ
μάρτυς, μάρτυρος, ὁ; dative plural μάρτυσιν
μήν, μηνός, ὁ
νύξ, νυκτός, ἡ
παῖς, παιδός, ὁ or ἡ
πούς, ποδός, ὁ
σάρξ, σαρκός, ἡ
Σίμων, Σίμωνος, ὁ
σωτήρ, σωτῆρος, ὁ; dative plural σωτῆρσιν
χάρις, χάριτος, ἡ; accusative singular χάριν
χείρ, χειρός, ἡ; dative plural χερσίν

The following five so-called 'relationship nouns' have some irregular inflections, and some irregular accents as well. These must be memorized. Note that the vocative is included as a separate form. With most third declension nouns, the nominative does double duty as the vocative as well; but the important exceptions (including the following) must be carefully observed.

Sing.					
N.	ἀνήρ	γυνή	θυγάτηρ	μήτηρ	πατήρ
V.	ἄνερ	γύναι	θύγατερ	μήτηρ	πάτερ
A.	ἄνδρα	γυναῖκα	θυγατέρα	μητέρα	πατέρα
G.	ἀνδρός	γυναικός	θυγατρός	μητρός	πατρός
D.	ἀνδρί	γυναικί	θυγατρί	μητρί	πατρί

Plur.					
N.	ἄνδρες	γυναῖκες	θυγατέρες	μητέρες	πατέρες
A.	ἄνδρας	γυναῖκας	θυγατέρας	μητέρας	πατέρας
G.	ἀνδρῶν	γυναικῶν	θυγατέρων	μητέρων	πατέρων
D.	ἀνδράσιν	γυναιξίν	θυγατράσιν	μητράσιν	πατράσιν

Exercise

1. και ἐγειρεσθε ταις χερσιν της γυναικος.
2. φυλασσεσθωσαν οἱ παιδες ὑπο των Ἑλληνων.
3. γυναι, μη εὑρες ἱκανον ἀργυριον τοις ἀρχουσιν;
4. ἀλλα καλαι θυγατερες γενησονται ὁμοιαι ταις μητρασιν αὐτων.
5. ἀπηγγειλαμεν δε ὁτι ἐστιν σωτηρ ταις γυναιξιν.
6. οὐ μενουσιν (future) ἐν τῃ γῃ αὐτων εἱς των αὐτων;
7. ἰδε, ὦ γυναι, οἱ των οὐρανων ἀστερες μαρτυρουσιν τῳ Σωτηρι.
8. μετα το ἀποθανειν τον πατερα αὐτου κατῳκησεν ἐν τῃ γῃ ταυτῃ.
9. και αὐτην ἀπεκτεινεν τοις ποσιν της εἰκονος ἡ ἐπεσεν ἐν μεσῳ του ναου.
10. ὁ σωτηρ ἐστιν ὑπερ τον διδασκαλον, ὁτι ἀπεθανεν ὑπερ των προβατων.

Third Declension Neuter Nouns

First Type

The first type of third declension neuter noun offers no special difficulty as far as accent is concerned. The rules already established are carefully followed. To give four examples:

Sing.	**N.**	σῶμα	πνεῦμα	θέλημα	φῶς
	A.	σῶμα	πνεῦμα	θέλημα	φῶς
	G.	σώματος	πνεύματος	θελήματος	φωτός
	D.	σώματι	πνεύματι	θελήματι	φωτί
Plur.	**N.**	σώματα	πνεύματα	θελήματα	φῶτα
	A.	σώματα	πνεύματα	θελήματα	φῶτα
	G.	σωμάτων	πνευμάτων	θελημάτων	φωτῶν
	D.	σώμασιν	πνεύμασιν	θελήμασιν	φωσίν

Second Type

The second type of third declension neuter noun at first sight has accentuation as strange as its inflection. For example:

Sing.	**N.**	γένος
	A.	γένος
	G.	γένους
	D.	γένει
Plur.	**N.**	γένη
	A.	γένη
	G.	γενῶν
	D.	γένεσιν

When the accentuation is reckoned on the basis of the stem γενες, which has suffered the loss of the final ς and undergone contraction, the accents are fully comprehensible. For example:

Sing. N.A.	——	
G.	γένε(σ)+ος	→ γένους
D.	γένε(σ)+ι	→ γένει
Plur. N.A.	γένε(σ)+α	→ γένη
G.	γενέ(σ)+ων	→ γενῶν
D.	γένε(σ)+σιν	→ γένεσιν

In short, the accents are generated in the same way they are generated in -εω verbs. This leads to the following rule:

NR.13 Third declension neuter nouns of the second (-ες stem) type adhere, in all inflections except the nominative/accusative singular, to *VR.2* (including *VR.2.1* and *VR.2.2*).

Three more examples may be of use:

Sing. N.	ἔθνος	ἔλεος	πλῆθος
A.	ἔθνος	ἔλεος	πλῆθος
G.	ἔθνους	ἐλέους	πλήθους
D.	ἔθνει	ἐλέει	πλήθει
Plur. N.	ἔθνη	ἐλέη	πλήθη
A.	ἔθνη	ἐλέη	πλήθη
G.	ἐθνῶν	ἐλεῶν	πληθῶν
D.	ἔθνεσιν	ἐλεείσιν	πλήθεσιν

Properly accented vocabulary of third declension neuter nouns of the *first* type which should be memorized includes:[1]

αἷμα	οὖς, ὠτός	στόμα
βάπτισμα	πνεῦμα	σῶμα
θέλημα	πῦρ, πυρός	τέρας, τέρατος
κρίμα	ῥῆμα	ὕδωρ, ὕδατος
ὄνομα	σπέρμα	φῶς, φωτός

Properly accented vocabulary of third declension neuter nouns of the *second* type which should be memorized includes:

___

1. The genitive singular is -ματος unless otherwise specified.

γένος	μέλος	σκεῦος
ἔθνος	μέρος	σκότος
ἔλεος	ὄρος	τέλος
ἔτος	πλῆθος	

To these we now add the indeclinable nouns (τὸ) πάσχα and (ὁ) Ἀβραάμ.

Exercise

1. ἔξομεν ἀρα βαπτισμα μετανοιας δια του αἱματος αὐτου;
2. ἰσχυρα δε ῥηματα κριματος ἐξηλθεν ἐκ του στοματος σου.
3. εἰπεν οὐν ὅτι οὐκ ἐστιν το φως, ἀλλ ' ἐρχεται μαρτυρησαι περι του φωτος.
4. μετα ταυτα ἡψατο του ὠτος τῃ χειρι αὐτου.
5. και διηλθομεν δια πυρος και ὑδατος, το γαρ πνευμα του ἐλεους κατῳκει ἡμας.
6. ἀνοιξει δε τα ὠτα των πληθων ἁ οὐ δυναται ἀκουειν.
7. ἰδετε τας χειρας και τους ποδας μου.
8. μη δυνανται οἱ ποδες εἰπειν ταις χερσιν ὅτι Χρειαν ὑμων οὐκ ἐχομεν, ὅτι οὐκ ἐστε μελη του σωματος;
9. ἐβαλεν δε το σπερμα εἰς σκευος ἐν τῃ ἡμερᾳ του πασχα.
10. και ἐσται τερατα ἐν τῳ σκοτει της νυκτος, αἱμα και πυρ και φοβος.

Third Declension Adjectives; Interrogative and Indefinite Pronouns

Third Declension Adjectives: First Type

AR.3 Third declension adjectives adopt accent patterns like those laid down for nouns in *NR.1*, *NR.4* and *NR.10*.

Comment: This rule must be carefully distinguished from *AR.1* (Lesson 8). Once *AR.3* is observed, if the accent of the masculine (= feminine) nominative singular form is known, the rest of the accents can be deduced. Two examples follow:

	M and F	N	M and F	N
Sing. N.	πλείων	πλεῖον	μείζων	μεῖζον
A.	πλείονα	πλεῖον	μείζονα	μεῖζον
G.	πλείονος	πλείονος	μείζονος	μείζονος
D.	πλείονι	πλείονι	μείζονι	μείζονι
Plur. N.	πλείονες	πλείονα	μείζονες	μείζονα
A.	πλείονας	πλείονα	μείζονας	μείζονα
G.	πλειόνων	πλειόνων	μειζόνων	μειζόνων
D.	πλείοσιν	πλείοσιν	μείζοσιν	μείζοσιν

Adjectives which follow these patterns include σώφρων, κρείσσων and χείρων.

Third Declension Adjectives: Second Type

AR.4 Third declension adjectives of the second (-ες stem) type adhere, in all inflections except the nominative masculine/feminine singular, to *VR.2* (including *VR.2.1* and *VR.2.2*).

Comment: Just as the accents of third declension nouns of the -ες stem type could be understood by referring to the contractions that had gone on, so similarly can the accents of third declension adjectives of the -ες stem type be understood. The one exception specified in *AR.4* must be carefully noted. It is only to be expected: the nominative masculine/feminine singular is highly erratic in the third declension and is in any case automatically learned as the new word is learned. Note that the accusative masculine/feminine plural is extraordinary. As the paradigm below reveals, this accusative masculine/feminine plural is identical to the nominative masculine/feminine plural—something which normally takes place only in the neuter gender.

		M and F	N
Sing.	*N.*	ἀληθής	ἀληθές
	A.	ἀληθῆ	ἀληθές
	G.	ἀληθοῦς	ἀληθοῦς
	D.	ἀληθεῖ	ἀληθεῖ
Plur.	*N.*	ἀληθεῖς	ἀληθῆ
	A.	ἀληθεῖς	ἀληθῆ
	G.	ἀληθῶν	ἀληθῶν
	D.	ἀληθέσιν	ἀληθέσιν

Or, to show more clearly how these accents have developed:

		M and F		N	
Sing.	*N.*	———		ἀληθέ(σ)	→ ἀληθές
	A.	ἀληθέ(σ)+α	→ ἀληθῆ	ἀληθέ(σ)	→ ἀληθές
	G.	ἀληθέ(σ)+ος	→ ἀληθοῦς	ἀληθέ(σ)+ος	→ ἀληθοῦς
	D.	ἀληθέ(σ)+ι	→ ἀληθεῖ	ἀληθέ(σ)+ι	→ ἀληθεῖ
Plur.	*N.*	ἀληθέ(σ)+ες	→ ἀληθεῖς	ἀληθέ(σ)+α	→ ἀληθῆ
	A.	———		ἀληθέ(σ)+α	→ ἀληθῆ
	G.	ἀληθέ(σ)+ων	→ ἀληθῶν	ἀληθέ(σ)+ων	→ ἀληθῶν
	D.	ἀληθέ(σ)+σιν	→ ἀληθέσιν	ἀληθέ(σ)+σιν	→ ἀληθέσιν

Chapter 22

95

Adjectives which follow this pattern include (besides ἀληθής) ἀσθενής and πλήρης. The latter, although it is not oxytone like the paradigm ἀληθής, can be accented from first principles by observing the regular rules of contraction. For convenience, the result is printed here:

		M and F	N
Sing.	*N*	πλήρης	πλῆρες
	A.	πλήρη	πλῆρες
	G.	πλήρους	πλήρους
	D.	πλήρει	πλήρει
Plur.	*N.*	πλήρεις	πλήρη
	A.	πλήρεις	πλήρη
	G.	πληρῶν	πληρῶν
	D.	πλήρεσιν	πλήρεσιν

In fact, there is evidence that in the first century AD, πλήρης, although normally declined as above, was sometimes treated as an indeclinable.

There is also one New Testament noun which follows the declined forms and accentuation of the adjective ἀληθής exactly: viz. (ὁ) συγγενής. The explanation for this is that the word was properly an adjective, 'related', before it came to function as the noun 'relative' or 'kinsman'.

Interrogative and Indefinite Pronouns

PR.2 The interrogative pronoun τίς in all its declensional forms *always* has an acute accent on the first syllable; and the indefinite pronoun τις is an enclitic.

		M and F	N
Sing.	*N.*	τίς	τί
	A.	τίνα	τί
	G.	τίνος	τίνος
	D.	τίνι	τίνι
Plur.	*N.*	τίνες	τίνα
	A.	τίνας	τίνα
	G.	τίνων	τίνων
	D.	τίσιν	τίσιν

Comment: This is an extraordinary rule, because the 'always' is taken absolutely. Even *GR.6* is overridden: i.e., in monosyllabic forms, τίς remains oxytone even when it is followed by another word and *GR.6* requires that the accent become a grave.

The indefinite pronoun corresponding to this is an enclitic in all declensional forms. (Review Lesson 9.) In normal usage, therefore, the indefinite pronoun will have no accent at all. When the accent is *retained* (as sometimes happens in the disyllabic forms), it will be an acute on the ultima (grave if followed by another word; see *GR.6*) except for the genitive plural τινων, which then has a circumflex accent on the ultima. Both the monosyllabic and all the disyllabic forms (including the genitive plural) can have an acute accent on the ultima if the enclitic is followed by another enclitic: review *EPR.5*, Lesson 9. For instance:

καί ἐάν τίς μου ἀκούσῃ τῶν ῥημάτων (John 12:47)
ἵνα τίς σε ἐρωτᾷ (John 16:30)
δυνατοὶ συγκαταβάντες εἴ τί ἐστιν ἐν τῷ ἀνδρὶ κτλ.[1] (Acts 25:5)

When the (enclitic) indefinite pronoun thus gains an acute accent, it is differentiable from the interrogative pronoun in all disyllabic forms because a different syllable is accented: e.g., τίνα and τινά. When, however, it is a monosyllabic form of the (enclitic) indefinite pronoun which has an acute accent, it is indistinguishable from the corresponding interrogative pronoun, apart from context.

PR.3 The indefinite relative pronoun ὅστις follows the basic noun rule *NR.1*, but also *EPR.9*.

Comment: The only forms that occur in the New Testament are: the nominative singular and plural of all genders (ὅστις, ἥτις, ὅτι; οἵτινες, αἵτινες, ἅτινα); the accusative neuter singular and plural (ὅτι and ἅτινα, identical with the neuter nominatives); and the old Attic genitive singular ὅτου (properly οὗτινος). But these forms are enough to reveal how important *PR.3* is. For instance, ἥτις is ordinarily inconceivable, according to *GR.5*; but an exception is made because the word is a compound, the second part of it an enclitic. Therefore the compound, like ὥσπερ, is accented as if the enclitic were a separate word (*EPR.9*; *EPR.5*). Each accent on the first part of the compound indefinite relative pronoun is exactly what it is on the relative pronoun.

---

1. κτλ (καὶ τὰ λοιπά) is approximately equivalent to *etc.*

Exercise

1. παραληψονται δε μισθον ός έστιν κρεισσων της ζωης.
2. Άβρααμ, ή δικαιοσυνη σου περισσευει, ότι έστιν πλειων της δικαιοσυνης του γενους σου.
3. και τινες των Φαρισαιων είπαν έν έαυτοις, Τι βλασφημει;
4. τι σοι δοκει, Σιμων; συ τινα με λεγεις είναι;
5. οί δε άληθεις πρεσβυτεροι έν άλεει παρακαλουσιν τα άσθενη παιδια
   αύτων.
6. τι με πειραζεις, ύποκριτα; τινος έστιν ή είκων αύτη;
7. δυναται τις είσελθειν είς την οίκιαν του ίσχυρου;
8. ό δε άδελφος σου έχει τι κατα σου.
9. λαλουσιν τινες κατα σαρκα, άλλα το Πνευμα έστιν κατα της σαρκος.
10. ούτοι είσιν οί άνθρωποι οίτινες άκουουσιν τα ρηματα του πληθους.

Third Declension Nouns with Vowel Stems

Stems Ending in -υ

There is only one special problem in accent for third declension nouns ending in υ, and it is not serious. Consider the word ἰχθύς, fully declined:

Sing. N.	(ὁ) ἰχθύς
A.	ἰχθύν
G.	ἰχθύος
D.	ἰχθύϊ
Plur. N.	ἰχθύες
A.	ἰχθύας
G.	ἰχθύων
D.	ἰχθύσιν

But some think the correct accentuation is ὁ ἰχθῦς, with corresponding adjustments where such are made necessary by the various inflectional endings. Similar doubt exists for some of the other eight New Testament words which follow this paradigm: ὁ στάχυς, ἡ ὀσφύς, τὸ (δάκρυ-: only in genitive and dative plural in the New Testament), ἡ ὀφρύς, ὁ βότρυς, ἡ ἀχλύς, ἡ ἰσχυς, ἡ ὑς. But as no change in the rules is required by such debates, we may ignore them until Lesson 37. For our purposes, we shall use only ἰχθύς in the exercises, and in the form provided above.

Stems Ending in -ι

NR.14 Nouns ending with -ις in the nominative singular and -εως in the genitive singular constitute a major exception to the rule that if the ultima is long the antepenult cannot be accented (*GR.4.1*); and this only in the genitive singular and plural.

Comment: The prolonged identification of these words in the rule just given distinguishes them from third declension words such as ἐλπίς, with which they are easily confused. But the stem of ἐλπίς is ἐλπίδ-; its genitive singular is ἐλπίδος. The words with which *NR.14* is concerned are like πόλις, with genitive singular πόλεως: their stem ends in ι, like πόλι-.

The application of *NR.14* to πολις is straightforward. Note especially the genitive singular and plural.

Sing. N.	πόλις	
A.	πόλις	
G.	πόλεως	
D.	πόλει	
Plur. N.	πόλεις	
A.	πόλεις	
G.	πόλεων	
D.	πόλεσιν	

In some words of this type, however, the accent in the nominative singular is on the antepenult, not (as in πόλις) on the penult. Alternatively, the word is properispomenon, not proparoxytone. In these instances it is important to observe what *NR.14* does and does not require. To take two examples:

Sing. N.	ἀποκάλυψις	γνῶσις
A.	ἀποκάλυψιν	γνῶσιν
G.	ἀποκαλύψεως	γνώσεως
D.	ἀποκαλύψει	γνώσει
Plur. N.	ἀποκαλύψεις	γνώσεις
A.	ἀποκαλύψεις	γνώσεις
G.	ἀποκαλύψεων	γνώσεων
D.	ἀποκαλύψεσιν	γνώσεσιν

In ἀποκάλυψις, for instance, the accent moves one syllable toward the end in the genitive singular ἀποκαλύψεως; but this is because, had it not done so, it would have been on the *fourth* syllable from the end. The accent does not have to move at all in πόλις; it does have to move in ἀποκάλυψις. The forms ἀποκαλύψεως and ἀποκαλύψεων are in strict conformity with *NR.14*, and therefore rightly in contravention of *GR.4.1*. In the dative singular, the accent remains on the *υ* and does not return to the *a*, because *NR.14* allows an exception to *GR.4.1 only* in the genitive of both numbers, not in the dative. Similar comments could be made for all the accents, and the student should be certain that he understands and can explain each accent in the above forms.

Third declension nouns of this type whose accents should now be noted include:

ἀνάστασις	δύναμις	πίστις
ἀποκάλυψις	θλῖψις[1]	πόλις
ἄφεσις	κρίσις	συνείδησις
γνῶσις	παράδοσις	

All of these nouns are feminine. In the New Testament there is one masculine noun which declines exactly the same way, viz. *ὁ ὄφις*; and there is one neuter noun which is almost the same, but which occurs only in the singular:

Sing. N.	*(τὸ) σίναπι*
A.	*σίναπι*
G.	*σινάπεως*
D.	*σινάπει*

Stems Ending in -ευ

Third declension nouns of this sort are all masculine, and all are oxytones in the nominative singular. Observe that the accent remains on the same syllable, as counted from the beginning of the word, in all declined forms.

Sing. N.	*βασιλεύς*
V.	*βασιλεῦ*
A.	*βασιλέα*
G.	*βασιλέως*
D.	*βασιλεῖ*
Plur. N.	*βασιλεῖς*
A.	*βασιλεῖς*
G.	*βασιλέων*
D.	*βασιλεῦσιν*

1. Some editors prefer *θλίψις*.

Other words of this type which should be noted are *γραμματεύς*, *ἱερεύς* and *ἀρχιερεύς*. All such nouns are masculine.

Stems Ending in *-ου*

The inflection of third declension nouns ending in *-ου* is slightly irregular, but the accent is regular. For example:

Sing.	*N.*	*βοῦς*
	A.	*βοῦν*
	G.	*βοός*
	D.	*βοΐ*
Plur.	*N.*	*βόες*
	A.	*βόας*
	G.	*βοῶν*
	D.	*βουσίν*

Exercise

1. *καὶ οἱ ἄνδρες περιεπατουν ἐν ταις πολεσιν συν ταις γυναιξιν αὐτου.*
2. *παρηγγειλεν οὖν ταις ἰδιαις θυγατρασιν ἑτοιμασαι τον ἰχθυν τῳ βασιλει.*
3. *καὶ δει τους γραμματεις λαβειν τους ἰχθυας ἐκ του ὑδατος τοις ἱερευσιν.*
4. *καὶ ἐθαυμαζον ὅτι μετα του ἀρχιερεως ἐλαλει.*
5. *οὑτοι εἰσιν οἱ ἀνθρωποι οἱτινες λεγουσιν ἀναστασιν μη εἰναι.*
6. *καὶ ἐσται χειρων χρονος κρισεως και θλιψεως.*
7. *αἱ δε των ἀνθρωπων παραδοσεις οὐκ ἀξουσιν την ἀφεσιν των ἁμαρτιων.*
8. *καὶ διωξουσιν ὑμας ἀπο πολεως εἰς πολιν.*
9. *ὁ γαρ μαθητης οὐ φιλει πατερα και μητερα ὑπερ ἐμε.*
10. *ἐγω γαρ παρα ἀνθρωπου οὐ παρελαβον αὐτο, ἀλλα δι᾽ ἀποκαλυψεως.*

Adjectives and Pronouns of the Third and First Declensions; Numerals

AR.5 Mixed third and first declension adjectives normally adhere to *A R.3*, and also to the accent pattern of *NR.11* and *NR.12*, in the masculine and neuter genders; but they follow the accent pattern of first declension *nouns* (not adjectives!) in the feminine gender.

Comment: Consider the accents on the full declension of πᾶς (which of course can serve as either adjective or pronoun):

	M	F	N
Sing. N.	πᾶς	πᾶσα	πᾶν
A.	πάντα	πᾶσαν	πᾶν
G.	παντός	πάσης	παντός
D.	παντί	πάσῃ	παντί
Plur. N.	πάντες	πᾶσαι	πάντα
A.	πάντας	πάσας	πάντα
G.	πάντων	πασῶν	πάντων
D.	πᾶσιν	πάσαις	πᾶσιν

This word follows the rule fairly closely. πᾶς is monosyllabic; and therefore an oxytone παντός etc. is expected (cf. *NR.11*). But paroxytone πάντων in the masculine and neuter genders is an exception which must be noted. (This is the second such exception: cf. παίδων, Lesson 20.) The fact that πᾶσιν (dative plural, masculine and neuter) is not oxytone contravenes *NR.11*; but granted the exception, then the accent on πᾶσιν nicely follows *NR.12*. Note, however, that the long vowel of the nominative has become short throughout masculine and neuter forms until the dative plural: there is no rule to cover this strange shortening. The long vowel is retained throughout the feminine gender. The two features which reveal that the accent throughout the feminine forms follows the pattern of first declension *nouns*, rather than first declension *adjectives*, are: (1) the short final *a* in nominative and accusative singular (contrast *AR.2*); and (2) the circumflex on the ultima of the genitive plural (cf. *NR.5*).

This word has a slightly more literary alternative spelling: ἅπας, ἅπασα, ἅπαν. This form follows *AR.5* exactly.

	M	F	N
Sing. N.	ἅπας	ἅπασα	ἅπαν
A.	ἅπαντα	ἅπασαν	ἅπαν
G.	ἅπαντος	ἁπάσης	ἅπαντος
D.	ἅπαντι	ἁπάσῃ	ἅπαντι
Plur. N.	ἅπαντες	ἅπασαι	ἅπαντα
A.	ἅπαντας	ἁπάσας	ἅπαντα
G.	ἁπάντων	ἁπασῶν	ἁπάντων
D.	ἅπασιν	ἁπάσαις	ἅπασιν

Similarly, the adjective ταχύς, despite some unusual inflections, is perfectly regular as far as accents are concerned:

	M	F	N
Sing. N.	ταχύς	ταχεῖα	ταχύ
A.	ταχύν	ταχεῖαν	ταχύ
G.	ταχέως	ταχείας	ταχέως
D.	ταχεῖ	ταχείᾳ	ταχεῖ
Plur. N.	ταχεῖς	ταχεῖαι	ταχέα
A.	ταχεῖς	ταχείας	ταχέα
G.	ταχέων	ταχειῶν	ταχέων
D.	ταχέσιν	ταχείαις	ταχέσιν

The cardinal 'one' follows *AR.5* also, but has one anomaly: the accent shifts to the ultima even in the feminine of the genitive and dative (singular; there is of course no plural):

	M	F	N
Sing. N.	εἷς	μία	ἕν
A.	ἕνα	μίαν	ἕν
G.	ἑνός	μιᾶς	ἑνός
D.	ἑνί	μιᾷ	ἑνί

The same is true for *οὐδείς* and *μηδείς*:

	M	F	N
Sing. N.	οὐδείς	οὐδεμία	οὐδέν
A.	οὐδένα	οὐδεμίαν	οὐδέν
G.	οὐδενός	οὐδεμιᾶς	οὐδενός
D.	οὐδενί	οὐδεμιᾷ	οὐδενί

	M	F	N
Sing. N.	μηδείς	μηδεμία	μηδέν
A.	μηδένα	μηδεμίαν	μηδέν
G.	μηδενός	μηδεμιᾶς	μηδεμιᾶς
D.	μηδενί	μηδεμιᾷ	μηδεμιᾷ

To these we may add two irregular but very common adjectives. In the masculine and neuter they change their stem in the genitive singular, and similarly throughout the feminine gender. The accentuation for all forms with longer stems is precisely the same as that for second and first declension adjectives (cf. *AR.1*). This means, among other things, that the genitive plural of the feminine does not automatically receive a circumflex accent (an observation relevant to the second word, not the first). It may be helpful as a mnemonic device to note that the first word is always accented on the ultima, and the second always has an acute accent on the penult.

	M	F	N
Sing. N.	πολύς	πολλή	πολύ
A.	πολύν	πολλήν	πολύ
G.	πολλοῦ	πολλῆς	πολλοῦ
D.	πολλῷ	πολλῇ	πολλῷ
Plur. N.	πολλοί	πολλαί	πολλά
A.	πολλούς	πολλάς	πολλά
G.	πολλῶν	πολλῶν	πολλῶν
D.	πολλοῖς	πολλαῖς	πολλοῖς

	M	F	N
Sing. N.	μέγας	μεγάλη	μέγα
A.	μέγαν	μεγάλην	μέγα
G.	μεγάλου	μεγάλης	μεγάλου
D.	μεγάλῳ	μεγάλῃ	μεγάλῳ
Plur. N.	μεγάλοι	μεγάλαι	μεγάλα
A.	μεγάλους	μεγάλας	μεγάλα
G.	μεγάλων	μεγάλων	μεγάλων
D.	μεγάλοις	μεγάλαις	μεγάλοις

Numerals

We have already come across the ordinals πρῶτος, δεύτερος, and τρίτος; and the cardinal εἷς was declined above. The following list of numerals does not exhaust those used in the New Testament, but includes representatives of different sorts, especially the most frequent ones:

δύο.   Indeclinable apart from dative plural δυσίν.

τρεῖς.[1]   Declined and accented as follows:

	M and F	N
N.A.	τρεῖς	τρία
G.	τριῶν	τριῶν
D.	τρισίν	τρισίν

τέσσαρες.   Declined and accented as follows:

	M and F	N
N.	τέσσαρες	τέσσαρα
A.	τέσσαρας	τέσσαρα
G.	τεσσάρων	τεσσάρων
D.	τέσσαρσιν	τέσσαρσιν

πέντε.   Indeclinable—as are all the numbers from 5 to 100, some of which are given here.

ἕξ	6
ἑπτά	7
ὀκτώ	8
ἐννέα	9
δέκα	10
ἕνδεκα	11
δώδεκα	12
εἴκοσιν	20
τεσσαράκοντα	40
ἑκατόν	100

χίλιοι, -αι, -α.   This is the cardinal for 'thousand'. It is a normal second and first declension (plural) adjective.

1. Note that τρεῖς is monosyllabic: cf. NR.11.

χιλιάς, -αδος, ἡ.   This third declension collective noun treats 'one thousand' as a unit. It declines and is accented normally.

From ἑκατόν and χίλιοι come the following two military ranks:

> ὁ ἑκαντοντάρχης
> ὁ χιλίαρχος

Adverbials occur in the New Testament for the numerals 1, 2, 3, 4, 5, 7 and 70. Naturally, they are indeclinable; and so the position of their accent is also fixed:

> ἅπαξ
> δίς
> τρίς
> τετράκις
> πεντάκις
> ἑπτάκις
> ἑβδομηκοντάκις

Note: Although verbal forms have not been given in the vocabularies of this *Manual* because their accents are normally deducible from first principles, nevertheless the correct accents of all other words used in the exercises have to this point been provided, at least in the nominative singular whence other accents are deducible. From now on the exercises will progressively introduce vocabulary not mentioned in the lessons. This will require that the student check a lexicon for the accentuation of these words. The rules already presented are sufficient to fix the accent in any declensional form; and the key at the back of the *Manual* continues to provide the student with a means to check his work. More and more sentences in the exercises are direct quotations from the New Testament.

Exercise

1. οἱ τεσσαρες λησται ἐφυγον εἰς τα ὀρη.
2. οἱ ἑξ ἱερεις ἠλθον νυκτος και ἠραν τα σωματα των τριων προφητων.
3. ἀνοιξεις δε τα στοματα ἡμων, Κυριε, και πασα γλωσσα εὐλογησει το μεγα ὀνομα σου.
4. μη βασταζετε μηδενα εἰς την συναγωγην ἐν τῳ σαββατῳ.
5. και παντες οἱ μαθηται πληρεις πιστεως ἠσαν και του Ἁγιου Πνευματος, και ἐθεραπευσαν τους ἀσθενεις και ἐξεβαλον πολλα δαιμονια.

6. μηδεις σκανδαλιζετω ἑνα των παιδων τουτων.

7. ἑν δε ἑκεινῃ τῃ ὡρᾳ συναγονται προς αὑτον πολλοι των ἀρχιερεων οἱ λεγουσιν ὁτι οὑκ ἑσται ἀναστασις.

8. ὁ δε ἑκατονταρχης ἀπεκρινατο, Ἐγω εἱμι ἀνθρωπος ὑπο ἑξουσιαν και ἑχω ἑκατον στρατιωτας ὑπ᾽ ἑμε.

9. ὁτε ἡλθον εἱς τας ἑξ κωμας ἑκηρυξαν το εὑαγγελιον πασιν τοις ἑθνεσιν ἁ κατῳκει ἑν αὑταις.

10. ὁ χιλιαρκος και χιλιοι ἀνδρες περιεπατουν ἑν ταις τρισιν πολεσιν.

Comparison of Adjectives; Adverbs

Comparison of Adjectives

AR.6 Those comparative and superlative adjectives which are formed by substituting -*τερος* and -*τατος* respectively for the final *ς* of the nominative masculine singular form of second and first declension adjectives follow *AR.1* and *AR.2*.

Comment: It may be helpful to provide a detailed example:

	M	F	N
Sing. N.	δικαιότερος	δικαιοτέρα	δικαιότερον
A.	δικαιότερον	δικαιοτέραν	δικαιότερον
G.	δικαιοτέρου	δικαιοτέρας	δικαιοτέρου
D.	δικαιοτέρῳ	δικαιοτέρᾳ	δικαιοτέρῳ
Plur. N.	δικαιότεροι	δικαιότεραι	δικαιότερα
A.	δικαιοτέρους	δικαιοτέρας	δικαιότερα
G.	δικαιοτέρων	δικαιοτέρων	δικαιοτέρων
D.	δικαιοτέροις	δικαιοτέραις	δικαιοτέροις
Sing. N.	δικαιότατος	δικαιοτάτη	δικαιότατον
A.	δικαιότατον	δικαιοτάτην	δικαιότατον
G.	δικαιοτάτου	δικαιοτάτης	δικαιοτάτου
D.	δικαιοτάτῳ	δικαιοτάτῃ	δικαιοτάτῳ
Plur. N.	δικαιότατοι	δικαιόταται	δικαιότατα
A.	δικαιοτάτους	δικαιοτάτας	δικαιότατα
G.	δικαιοτάτων	δικαιοτάτων	δικαιοτάτων
D.	δικαιοτάτοις	δικαιοτάταις	δικαιοτάτοις

One very common irregular superlative adjective which also follows *A R.1* and *A R.2* is ἐλάχιστος, the superlative of μικρός (positive) and μικρότερος (comparative). A synonym for μικρότερος is the third and first declension adjective ἐλάσσων, declined and accented like κρείσσων, χείρων, μείζων and πλείων (Lesson 22).

Adverbs

IWR.3 Adverbs whose spelling is identical with a neuter accusative form of the corresponding adjective adopt the same accent as that of the borrowed form.

Comment: Several examples will illustrate the rule. From μόνος comes μόνον, which is the neuter accusative, but which also functions as the adverb 'only'. Similarly δικαιότερον is the neuter singular of the comparative adjective, but also the comparative adverb of δικαιῶς. From the adjective κρείσσων comes the neuter κρεῖσσον, which is also the adverb 'better'. In each case both the spelling *and the accentuation* remain the same.

IWR.4 Adverbs generated by replacing the ν of the genitive plural of an adjective with a ς retain the accent of the genitive plural adjective.

Comment: This is an extremely helpful rule, for it explains, for instance, why the adverb of σοφός is σοφῶς (σοφός → σοφῶν → σοφῶς) while the adverb of δίκαιος is δικαίως (δίκαιος → δικαίων →δικαίως). Similarly, ἀληθής generates ἀληθῶς, and οὗτος generates οὕτως (via τούτων; the spelling has changed, but not the accent).

The accent of the following adverbs should also be memorized at this stage:

> ἀμήν
> εὖ
> μάλιστα
> μᾶλλον
> ναί

Two further indeclinable words should be noted: the interjection οὐαί, and the comparative and disjunctive particle ἤ.

Exercise

1. γη Σοδομων ἀνεκτοτερον ἐσται ἐν ἡμερᾳ κρισεως ἡ σοι.
2. οὐαι, οὐχι ἡ ψυχη πλειον ἐστιν της τροφης;
3. ἰδου ἡ ἐλπις και ἡ ἀγαπη μειζονες εἰσιν της πιστεως, μαλιστα ἡ ἀγαπη.
4. ὁ νεωτερος των υἱων οὐκ ἠθελεν ἐργαζεσθαι ὑπερ του πατρος αὐτου.
5. αἱρει γαρ το πληρωμα αὐτου ἀπο του ἱματιου και χειρον σχισμα γινεται.
6. ἀμην λεγω ὑμιν Ὁτε ἐποιησατε ἑνι τουτων των ἀδελφων μου των ἐλαχιστων, ἐμοι ἐποιησατε.
7. ναι, ἀπεκτεινατε τον σοφωτατον των ἀνθρωπων.
8. ὁ δε ἐκραξεν μαλλον, Ἰδου πασχω ταις χερσιν των ἐχθρων μου.
9. λεγω ὑμιν Μειζων ἐν γεννητοις γυναικων Ἰωαννου οὐδεις ἐστιν· ὁ δε μικροτερος ἐν τῃ βασιλειᾳ του θεου μειζων αὐτου ἐστιν.
10. δει ἡμας ὑπακουειν τῳ βασιλει ἡ τῳ ἱερει.

Perfect and Pluperfect

Whatever difficulties attend the inflection of perfects and pluperfects, both active and middle/passive, no such problem attends their accent in the indicative: the basic verb (recessive) rule, *VR.1*, fixes the accent in every form. Moreover, the ambiguous length of the α in certain perfect active endings has already been declared short by *VR.5*. For convenience, the correctly accented paradigm verb is presented in the indicative:

Active		Middle/Passive	
Perfect	*Pluperfect*	*Perfect*	*Pluperfect*
λέλυκα	(ἐ)λελύκειν	λέλυμαι	(ἐ)λελύμην
λέλυκας	(ἐ)λελύκεις	λέλυσαι	(ἐ)λέλυσο
λέλυκεν	(ἐ)λελύκει	λέλυται	(ἐ)λέλυτο
λελύκαμεν	(ἐ)λελύκειμεν	λελύμεθα	(ἐ)λελύμεθα
λελύκατε	(ἐ)λελύκειτε	λέλυσθε	(ἐ)λέλυσθε
λελύκασιν	(ἐ)λελύκεισαν	λέλυνται	(ἐ)λέλυντο

The infinitives can be accented once the following is known:

VR.11 Both the perfect active infinitive and the perfect middle/passive infinitive have an acute accent on the penult.

Comment: Hence, λελυκέναι and λελύσθαι.

These patterns of accents hold true even for common New Testament verbs that are perfect in form but present in meaning, notably οἶδα (pluperfect ᾔδειν, infinitive εἰδέναι).

On pp. 146–48 of the *Manual*, there is a list of the principal parts of the most common New Testament irregular verbs, all properly accented. Because all of these parts follow the recessive rule (*VR.1*), the student ought to be able to deduce for himself where and what the accent should be. The accents have been provided, however, and should be properly pronounced as part of the routine recitation of these principal parts. For this lesson, study λύω and φιλέω, and then ἀγγέλλω to -θνήσκω, including also κηρύσσω and πράσσω.

Exercise

1. παιδια, ἐσχατη ὡρα ἐστιν, και καθως ἠκουσατε ὁτι ἀντιχριστος ἐρχεται, και νυν ἀντιχριστοι πολλοι γεγονασιν.
2. οὐ γεγραπται Ὁ οἰκος μου οἰκος προσευχης;
3. ὁ δε ἀπεκρινατο, Ὁ γεγραφα, γεγραφα.
4. Χριστος ἀπεθανεν και ἐγηγερται τῃ ἡμερᾳ τῃ τριτῃ.
5. οἱ δε τεσσαρες γραμματεις εὑρηκασιν παντα τα μεγαλα σκευη.
6. και ἠσαν ἀνθρωποι οἱτινες φονον πεποιηκεισαν.
7. θελω δε ὑμας εἰδεναι ὁτι παντος ἀνδρος ἡ κεφαλη ὁ Χριστος ἐστιν.
8. οὐδεις ἐδυνατο αὐτον δησαι, δια το αὐτον πολλακις δεδεσθαι.
9. πρωχος δε τις ὀνοματι Λαζαρος ἐβεβλητο προς τον πυλωνα αὐτου.
10. ὁ δε θεος λελαληκεν ταυτα τα ῥηματα εἰς το εἰδεναι ὑμας τις ἐστιν ἡ ἐλπις της κλησεως αὐτου.

Aorist and Future Passives

Whatever difficulties attend the inflections of aorist passives and future passives in the indicative mood (and, for the aorist passive, the imperative), once again the accent is completely determined by the recessive rule (*VR.1*).

For convenience, the correctly accented paradigm verb is included below in the first aorist passive indicative and imperative, and in the future passive indicative:

First Aorist Passive	
Indicative	*Imperative*
ἐλύθην	λύθητι
ἐλύθης	λυθήτω
ἐλύθη	λύθητε
ἐλύθημεν	λυθήτωσαν
ἐλύθητε	
ἐλύθησαν	

First Future Passive: Indicative:
λυθήσομαι
λυθήσῃ
λυθήσεται
λυθησόμεθα
λυθήσεσθε
λυθήσονται

The future passive exhibits no infinitive in the New Testament.

The aorist passive infinitive may always be correctly accented by observing the following rule:

VR.12 The aorist passive infinitive has a circumflex accent on the penult.

The accented table of irregular verbs (pp. 146–48) should be studied afresh, especially the verbs from καίω to φθείρω.

Exercise

1. πολλα των ῥηματων τουτων ἐγραφη ἐν βιβλιῳ ὑπο του ἀρχιερεως.
2. ἠχθη δε ὁ Ἰησους ὑπο του πνευματος εἰς τα ὁρη πειρασθηναι ὑπο του διαβολου.
3. οἱ νεκροι ἐγερθησονται ἐν τῃ ἡμερᾳ της κρισεως τῃ φωνῃ του ἀγγελου.
4. οἰδαμεν ὁτι τουτο το εὐαγγελιον κηρυχθησεται πασιν τοις ἐθνεσιν και πολλοι ἀκουσονται.
5. ἐν ἐκεινῃ τῃ ἡμερᾳ πολλα σωματα των ἁγιων ἠγερθη, και ἠλθεν εἰς την πολιν, και ὠφθη πολλοις.
6. παντες οἱ ἰχθυες ἐβληθησαν εἰς το ὑδωρ.
7. διδασκαλε, φιληθηση ὑπο παντος του ἐθνους.
8. οἱ δε νεανιαι ἐστραφησαν ἀπο των ἁμαρτιων αὐτων ὁτι φοβος μεγας εἰληφει αὐτους.
9. και πεπωκαμεν το ποτηριον της χαρας ὁ ἀπεσταλκεν ὁ θεος.
10. δια το ὀνομα μου ἀχθησεσθε εἰς βασιλεις και ἀρχοντας.

LESSON **28**

Participles; More Adverbs

Participles

Participles are *verbal adjectives*; and from the point of view of accentuation, they are best considered under the adjective rules.

Participles with Third and First Declension Endings

Participles with third and first declension endings all adhere to *AR.5*, which governs third and first declension adjectives. This fact does not tell you where the accent is in the nominative singular masculine. Once that is known, however, *AR.5* fixes the accent for all forms. Among other things, this means there is a short *a* in the feminine nominative and accusative singular, and a circumflex accent on the ultima of the feminine genitive plural (which, it will be remembered, follows first declension *noun* accent patterns, not first declension *adjective* patterns).

There are four types of participles with third and first declension endings:

Type 1: -ων -ουσα -ον

The most common example is the present active participle of verbs like λύω:

	M	F	N
Sing. N.	λύων	λύουσα	λῦον
A.	λύοντα	λύουσαν	λῦον
G.	λύοντος	λυούσης	λύοντος
D.	λύοντι	λυούσῃ	λύοντι
Plur. N.	λύοντες	λύουσαι	λύοντα
A.	λύοντας	λυούσας	λύοντα
G.	λυόντων	λυουσῶν	λυόντων
D.	λύουσιν	λυούσαις	λύουσιν

All that need be remembered are the accents on λύων and λῦον.

When a contract verb such as φιλέω is in present participle form, the rules of accentuation for contracting syllables are strictly applied. For example:

	M	F	N
Sing. N.	φιλῶν	φιλοῦσα	φιλοῦν
A.	φιλοῦντα	φιλοῦσαν	φιλοῦν
G.	φιλοῦντος	φιλούσης	φιλοῦντος
D.	φιλοῦντι	φιλούσῃ	φιλοῦντι
Plur. N.	φιλοῦντες	φιλοῦσαι	φιλοῦντα
A.	φιλοῦντας	φιλούσας	φιλοῦντα
G.	φιλούντων	φιλουσῶν	φιλούντων
D.	φιλοῦσιν	φιλούσαις	φιλοῦσιν

The present participle of εἰμί declines like λύων; but obviously the accent is distinctive:

	M	F	N
Sing. N.	ὤν	οὖσα	ὄν
A.	ὄντα	οὖσαν	ὄν
G.	ὄντος	οὔσης	ὄντος
D.	ὄντι	οὔσῃ	ὄντι
Plur. N.	ὄντες	οὖσαι	ὄντα
A.	ὄντας	οὔσας	ὄντα
G.	ὄντων	οὐσῶν	ὄντων
D.	οὖσιν	οὔσαις	οὖσιν

AR.7 All second aorist active participles have the same accent as the corresponding form of the present participle of εἰμί.

Hence, the second aorist participle of βάλλω is: βαλών βαλοῦσα βαλόν

Type 2: -ας -ασα -αν

This is used for the first aorist active participle of verbs like λύω. It declines exactly like πᾶς, πᾶσα, πᾶν. The latter word, however, exhibits a couple of deviations from the accent rule *AR.5* (cf. Lesson 24), which this participle does not follow; but the participle introduces an anomaly of its own: the acute on λύσας coupled with the circumflex on λῦσαν, indicating that the *a* in λύσας is *long* (this is always so: e.g., ἀκούσας).

	M	**F**	**N**
Sing. N.	λύσας	λύσασα	λῦσαν
A.	λύσαντα	λύσασαν	λῦσαν
G.	λύσαντος	λυσάσης	λύσαντος
D.	λύσαντι	λυσάσῃ	λύσαντι
Plur. N.	λύσαντες	λύσασαι	λύσαντα
A.	λύσαντας	λυσάσας	λύσαντα
G.	λυσάντων	λυσασῶν	λυσάντων
D.	λύσασιν	λυσάσαις	λύσασιν

Type 3: -εις -εισα -εν

Used for the first aorist passive participle of verbs like λύω, and for the second aorist active participle of verbs like γράφω, this type follows *A R.5* exactly. Note carefully however where the accent rests in the nominative, from which the accents for the fully declined participle may be deduced.

	M	**F**	**N**
Sing. N.	λυθείς	λυθεῖσα	λυθέν
A.	λυθέντα	λυθεῖσαν	λυθέν
G.	λυθέντος	λυθείσης	λυθέντος
D.	λυθέντι	λυθείσῃ	λυθέντι
Plur. N.	λυθέντες	λυθεῖσαι	λυθέντα
A.	λυθέντας	λυθείσας	λυθέντα
G.	λυθέντων	λυθεισῶν	λυθέντων
D.	λυθεῖσιν	λυθείσαις	λυθεῖσιν

Similarly for the second aorist participle passive of γράφω:

γραφείς	γραφεῖσα	γραφέν
etc.	etc.	etc.

Type 4: -ως -υια -ος

This is used for the first perfect active participle of verbs like λύω, and for the second perfect active participle of verbs like οἶδα. It follows *A R.5* exactly; but again, it is important to memorize where the accent rests in the nominative.

	M	F	N
Sing. N.	λελυκώς	λελυκυῖα	λελυκός
A.	λελυκότα	λελυκυῖαν	λελυκός
G.	λελυκότας	λελυκυίας	λελυκότας
D.	λελυκότι	λελυκυίᾳ	λελυκότι
Plur. N.	λελυκότες	λελυκυῖαι	λελυκότα
A.	λελυκότας	λελυκυίας	λελυκότα
G.	λελυκότων	λελυκυιῶν	λελυκότων
D.	λελυκόσιν	λελυκυίαις	λελυκόσιν

Similarly for the second perfect active participle of *οἶδα*:

εἰδώς	εἰδυῖα	εἰδός
etc.	etc.	etc.

Participles with Second and First Declension Endings

All participles with second and first declension inflections decline with the endings -μενος, -μενη, -μενον. They strictly adhere to *A R.1*. Therefore the feminine genitive plural does *not* automatically have a circumflex on the ultima.

As far as accents are concerned, these participles may be divided into two groups, according to a simple rule:

AR.8 In the present middle/passive, the first aorist middle, the second aorist middle, and the present of the irregular verb *δύναμαι*, the accent on the participle is recessive in every form; but in the perfect middle/passive, the accent of the participle is always on the penult.

Comment: Note that in the first grouping, *A R.8* does not say that the accent *cannot* be on the penult, but only that it *must* be recessive. A long ultima in the first grouping will require that the accent be on the penult—which is just where it must be in the second grouping.

Two detailed examples will clarify this rule. The present participle, middle/passive, of *λύω*, is declined and accented as follows:

	M	F	N
Sing. N.	λυόμενος	λυομένη	λυόμενον
A.	λυόμενον	λυομένην	λυόμενον
G.	λυομένου	λυομένης	λυομένου
D.	λυομένῳ	λυομένη	λυομένῳ
Plur. N.	λυόμενοι	λυόμεναι	λυόμενα
A.	λυομένους	λυομένας	λυόμενα
G.	λυομένων	λυομένων	λυομένων
D.	λυομένοις	λυομέναις	λυομένοις

Similarly, the first aorist middle participle:

λυσάμενος	λυσαμένη	λυσάμενον

Or the second aorist middle participle:

γενόμενος	γενομένη	γενόμενον

Or the present participle of δύναμαι:

δυνάμενος	δυναμένη	δυνάμενον

By contrast, the perfect middle/passive participle always accents the penult:

	M	F	N
Sing. N.	λελυμένος	λελυμένη	λελυμένον
A.	λελυμένον	λελυμένην	λελυμένον
G.	λελυμένου	λελυμένης	λελυμένου
D.	λελυμένῳ	λελυμένη	λελυμένῳ
Plur. N.	λελυμένοι	λελυμέναι	λελυμένα
A.	λελυμένους	λελυμένας	λελυμένα
G.	λελυμένων	λελυμένων	λελυμένων
D.	λελυμένοις	λελυμέναις	λελυμένοις

Adverbs

The accents of the following adverbs should now be noted:

Adverbs of Place	Adverbs of Time	Interrogative Adverbs
ὧδε	νῦν, or νυνί	πῶς
ἐκεῖ	ἤδη	ποῦ
ὅπου	ἄρτι	
ἐγγύς	τότε	
	πάντοτε	
	πάλιν	
	ἔτι	
	οὐκέτι	
	μηκέτι	
	εὐθύς	
	εὐθέως	
	σήμερον	

Also to be noted at this stage are three new words: the interrogative pronominal adjective ποῖος, -α, -ον; and the correlatives ὅσος, -η, -ον and τοιοῦτος, -αύτη, -οῦτο. All three are accented as might be expected.

Exercise A

1. καὶ παραγων παρα την θαλασσαν της Γαλιλαιας εἶδεν Σιμωνα.
2. καὶ ἦσαν οἱ φαγοντες τους ἀρτους πεντακισχιλιοι ἀνδρες.
3. πολλοι οὖν των τελωνων ἐβαπτισθησαν μετανοουντες ἀπο των ἁμαρτιων αὐτων.
4. ἀκουων δε Ἀνανιας τους λογους τουτους πεσων ἀπεθανεν, και ἐγενετο φοβος μεγας ἐπι παντας τους ἀκουοντας.
5. ἐφοβουμεθα δε μη πιστευοντες ὅτι το ἐλεος αὐτου ἀληθες ἐστιν.
6. οὗτος γαρ ἐστιν ὁ πεμφθεις ὑπο του βασιλεως.
7. καὶ ὤφθη αὐτοις Μωϋσης και Ἡλειας συνλαλουντες μετ᾽ αὐτου.
8. καὶ μη φοβεισθε ἀπο των ἀποκτεινοντων το σωμα, την δε ψυχην μη δυναμενων ἀποκτειναι· φοβεισθε μαλλον τον δυναμενον και ψυχην και σωμα ἀπολεσαι ἐν γεεννη.
9. πορευθεντες δε ἀπηγγειλεν τοις ἀρχιερευσιν ἁπαντα τα γενομενα.
10. ταυτην δε θυγατερα Ἀβρααμ οὖσαν, ἥν ἐδησεν ὁ Σατανας δεκα και ὀκτω ἐτη, οὐκ ἐδει λυθηναι τη ἡμερᾳ του σαββατου;

Exercise B

1. ἐγγὺς δὲ οὔσης Λύδδας τῇ Ἰόππῃ, οἱ μαθηταὶ ἀκούσαντες ὅτι Πέτρος ἐστιν ἐκει, ἀπεστειλαν δυο ἀνδρας προς αὐτον.

2. ἀλλα λημψεσθε δυναμιν σημερον, ἐλθοντος του ἁγιου πνευματος ἐφ᾽ ὑμας.

3. τῆς ἡμερας ἐγγισασης ὁ υἱος του ἀνθρωπου ἐλευσεται μετα των νεφελων του οὐρανου.

4. κρατουντος δε αὐτου την χειρα μου ἐδεξαμην δυναμιν περιπατειν.

5. και ἠν ὁ Ἰωαννης ἐνδεδυμενος τριχας καμηλου.

6. ἐγγιζοντων δε αὐτων τῇ πολει ὁλον το πληθος ἐχαιρεν λέγον, Μακαριος ὁ ἐρχομενος ἐν ὀνοματι του Κυριου.

7. ὡδε ἐν Ἱεροσολυμοις ἐστιν ὁ τοπος ὁπου προσκυνειν δει.

8. ὑπαγε εἰς τον οἰκον σου προς τους σους, και ἀπαγγειλον αὐτοις ὁσα ὁ Κυριος σοι πεποιηκεν.

9. πως εἰσηλθες ὡδε μη ἐχων ἐνδυμα γαμου;

10. και τοιαυταις παραβολαις πολλαις ἐλαλει αὐτοις τον λογον.

The Subjunctive Mood

VR.13 In the subjunctive mood, all accents of verbs in the omega system adhere to *VR.1* (the recessive rule) except the accents of the first aorist passive and the second aorist passive.

Comment: Observe that the -μι verbs are excluded. They will be treated later (cf. Lessons 32–35).

The present subjunctive active is:

> λύω
> λύῃς
> λύῃ
> λύωμεν
> λύητε
> λύωσιν

Exactly the same in ending and accentuation are the first aorist active (λύσω, etc.), the second aorist active (βάλω, etc.) and the subjunctive of εἴδω. Similarly, the present subjunctive middle/passive is:

> λύωμαι
> λύῃ
> λύηται
> λυώμεθα
> λύησθε
> λύωνται

and the same endings and accents are found in the first aorist middle (λύσωμαι, etc.) and second aorist middle (γένωμαι, etc.).

Contract verbs in -εω follow *VR.2* as well, and the resulting accents are predictable:

Present Subjunctive Active		Present Subjunctive Middle/Passive	
φιλέ+ω	→ φιλῶ	φιλέ+ωμαι	→ φιλῶμαι
φιλέ+ῃς	→ φιλῇς	φιλέ+ῃ	→ φιλῇ
φιλέ+ῃ	→ φιλῇ	φιλέ+ηται	→ φιλῆται
φιλέ+ωμεν	→ φιλῶμεν	φιλέ+ώμεθα	→ φιλώμεθα
φιλέ+ητε	→ φιλῆτε	φιλέ+ησθε	→ φιλῆσθε
φιλέ+ωσιν	→ φιλῶσιν	φιλέ+ωνται	→ φιλῶνται

The subjunctive of *εἰμί* is:

> ὦ
> ᾖς
> ᾖ
> ὦμεν
> ἦτε
> ὦσιν

Observe that this subjunctive, too, is recessive, and therefore the accent is specified for the plural forms. The singular forms might conceivably have had the acute accent; but in fact they do not, and this should be noted.

The exceptions specified in *VR.13* are the first aorist subjunctive passive and the second aorist subjunctive passive, which are conjugated and accented as follows:

λυθῶ	γραφῶ
λυθῇ	γραφῇς
λυθῇ	γραφῇ
λυθῶμεν	γραφῶμεν
λυθῆτε	γραφῆτε
λυθῶσιν	γραφῶσιν

The accents of the following indeclinable words, used frequently with the subjunctive mood, should be noted:

> ἵνα
> ὅπως
> ἄν
> ὅταν (i.e. ὅτε + ἄν)
> ἐάν

Exercise

1. ἐμον βρωμα ἐστιν ἵνα ποιω το θελημα του πεμψαντος με.
2. ἀμην λεγω ὑμιν ὅτι οὐ μη παρελθῃ ἡ γενεα αὑτη ἑως ἀν παντα ταυτα γενηται.
3. ἀγωμεν εἰς τας ἀλλας κωμας, ἵνα και ἐκει κηρυξω.
4. ὁς ἀν ἑν των τοιουτων παιδιων δεξηται ἐπι τῳ ὀνοματι μου, ἐμε δεχεται· και ὁς ἀν ἐμε δεχεται, οὐκ ἐμε δεχεται, ἀλλα τον ἀποστειλαντα με.
5. ὁ ἐαν δησῃς ἐπι της γης ἐσται δεδεμενον ἐν τοις οὐρανοις.
6. τι ποιησωμεν; μενωμεν ἐν ἁμαρτιᾳ ἵνα περισσευῃ ἡ χαρις;
7. παντοτε γαρ τους πτωχους ἐχετε, και ὁταν θελητε δυνασθε αὐτοις εὐ ποιησαι.
8. ὁπου ἐαν κηρυχθῃ το εὐαγγελιον τουτο ἐν ὁλῳ τῳ κοσμῳ, λαληθησεται και ὁ ἐποιησεν αὑτη.
9. και παρεκαλει αὐτους ἵνα μετ᾽ αὐτου ὡσιν, και ἐλεγον ὅτι Προσευχεσθε ἵνα μη ἐλθητε εἰς τειρασμον.
10. και τινες των ὡδε ὀντων οὐ μη γευσωνται θανατου ἑως ἀν ἰδωσιν τον υἱον του ἀνθρωπου.

LESSON 30

The Optative Mood

The optative mood is used relatively infrequently in the New Testament, so that a detailed treatment of accents in the optative, complete with paradigms, is neither necessary nor desirable at this point. The following two simple observations will help the student avoid virtually all errors in accenting optatives found in the New Testament: (1) Optatives, like other parts of the finite verb, are normally recessive. This is true, for instance, in Paul's much-used expression, μὴ γένοιτο, in the third person singular of the verb εἰμί (the only form of the optative of εἰμί found in the New Testament), viz. εἴη, and virtually every other New Testament form. (2) One important class of *apparent* non-recessive accents should be noted. In Lesson 1, the third preliminary definition was: 'Diphthongs are always considered *long*, except for αι and οι which are considered *short* when final.' It was then pointed out that this exception for final αι and οι *does not hold in the optative mood*. This exception is only *apparent*, however, since some contraction has taken place.

Apparent or not, it is an important exception when trying to understand certain New Testament accents. Consider I Thess. 3:12: ὑμᾶς δὲ ὁ Κύριος πλεονάσαι καὶ περισσεύσαι τῇ ἀγάπῃ εἰς ἀλλήλους καὶ εἰς πάντας κτλ. The two words πλεονάσαι and περισσεύσαι are shown by context to be optatives (not aorist infinitives nor aorist middle imperatives); and their accents are not anomalous because the αι diphthong ending is considered long in the optative mood.

Also to be noted at this juncture are the indeclinable words εἰ and εἴτε (= εἰ+τε). One must also distinguish between πότε, 'when', and the enclitic ποτέ, 'once', 'formerly'. From the latter also derive combinations such as ἤδη ποτέ, 'now at length', and μήποτε, 'lest . . . ever' or 'whether . . . never'.

Exercise

1. τι οὖν ἐρουμεν; ἐπιμενωμεν τῃ ἁμαρτιᾳ, ἱνα ἡ χαρις πλεονασῃ; μη γενοιτο.
2. το ἀργυριον σου συν σοι εἰη εἰς ἀπωλειαν.
3. ἐαν τις θελῃ το θελημα αὑτου ποιειν, γνωσεται περι της διδαχης.
4. εἰ ἠπιστησαν τινες, μη ἡ ἀπιστια αὑτων την πιστιν του θεου καταργησει; μη γενοιτο· γινεσθω δε ὁ θεος ἀληθης, πας δε ἀνθρωπος ψευστης.
5. παντα γαρ ὑμων ἐστιν, εἰτε Παυλος εἰτε Ἀπολλως εἰτε Κηφας, εἰτε κοσμος εἰτε ζωη εἰτε θανατος, παντα ὑμων, ὑμεις δε Χριστου, Χριστος δε θεου.
6. ἐν τῃ πρωτῃ μου ἀπολογιᾳ οὐδεις μοι παρεγενετο, ἀλλα παντες με ἐγκατελιπον· μη αὑτοις λογισθειη.
7. γεγραπται γαρ ἐν βιβλῳ ψαλμων ὁτι Την ἐπισκοπην αὑτου λαβοι ἑτερος.
8. ὁ γραμματευς ἐμεινεν ἐν τῳ ὁρει τεσσαρακοντα ἡμερας και τεσσαρακοντα νυκτας γραφων πασας τας ἐντολας του νομου.
9. ἐαν ἠδει ὁ οἰκοδεσποτης ποιᾳ φυλακῃ ὁ κλεπτης ἐπχεται, ἐγρηγορησεν ἀν.
10. και παντες διελογιζοντο ἐν ταις καρδιαις αὑτων περι του Ιωαννου μηποτε αὐτος εἰη ὁ Χριστος.

LESSON **31**

More on Contract Verbs:
Verbs in -*αω* and -*οω*

So far we have examined only -*εω* contract verbs (Lesson 4); but -*αω* and -*οω* contracts are scarcely less common. The accent rule for contract verbs, already adduced (viz., *VR.2*, including *VR.2.1* and *VR.2.2*), is rigorously applied to these contracts in the same tenses, voices and moods where it is applied to -*εω* verbs, and ignored elsewhere (i.e., when the vowel which normally contracts is lengthened instead: e.g., *φιλῶ*, but *φιλήσω*).

Although *VR.2* governs -*αω* and *οω* contracts, nevertheless certain ambiguities arise in these contracts which are not present in -*εω* verbs. These ambiguities are eliminated by the following two rules:

VR.14 In -*αω* contract verbs, if the contracted syllable centers on an *α* or an *ᾳ*, that syllable is long.

VR.15 In -*οω* contract verbs, *VR.2.2* overrides the exception which says the diphthongs *αι* and *οι* are short when final.

Comment: *VR.14* is helpful in forms such as *τιμᾶτε*. If the *α* were not long, it could not have the circumflex accent; and if it is long, in this configuration it must have the circumflex accent. When it is remembered that *τιμᾶτε* comes from *τιμά+ετε* → *τιμᾶτε*, then according to *VR.14* the ambiguity is resolved. *VR.15* is helpful in forms such as *φανεροῖ*. Normally a final *οι* is short; but because in this instance *οι* is the result of contracting syllables (*φανερό+ει* → *φανεροῖ*), and the contracted syllable is final, it must receive a circumflex accent in accordance with *VR.2.2*, even at the expense of the normal exception.

For convenience, the correctly accented forms of *τιμάω*, *δηλόω*, and *ζάω* (which exhibits certain peculiarities) are printed below in all contracted

127

inflections. The student should be able both to explain and to reproduce the accentuation. (ζάω is omitted where its form does not exist—as in the passive voice; or where it exhibits no irregularities, or does not exist in the New Testament—as in the imperfect indicative active [except ἔζων, Rom. 7:9].)

Present Indicative Active

τιμῶ	δηλῶ	ζῶ
τιμᾷς	δηλοῖς	ζῇς
τιμᾷ	δηλοῖ	ζῇ
τιμῶμεν	δηλοῦμεν	ζῶμεν
τιμᾶτε	δηλοῦτε	ζῆτε
τιμῶσιν	δηλοῦσιν	ζῶσιν

Present Active Imperative

τίμα	δήλου
τιμάτω	δηλούτω
τιμᾶτε	δηλοῦτε
τιμάτωσαν	δηλούτωσαν

Present Subjunctive Active

τιμῶ	δηλῶ	ζῶ
τιμᾷς	δηλοῖς	ζῇς
τιμᾷ	δηλοῖ	ζῇ
τιμῶμεν	δηλοῦμεν	ζῶμεν
τιμᾶτε	δηλοῦτε	ζῆτε
τιμῶσιν	δηλοῦσιν	ζῶσιν

i.e. all forms exactly the same as those in the present indicative.

Present Active Infinitive

τιμᾶν	δηλοῦν	ζῆν

Present Active Participle

τιμῶν, τιμῶσα, τιμῶν	δηλῶν, δηλοῦσα, δηλοῦν	ζῶν, ζῶσα, ζῶν

Imperfect Indicative Active

ἐτίμων	ἐδήλουν
ἐτίμας	ἐδήλους
ἐτίμα	ἐδήλου
ἐτιμῶμεν	ἐδηλοῦμεν
ἐτιμᾶτε	ἐδηλοῦτε
ἐτίμων	ἐδήλουν

Present Indicative Middle/Passive

τιμῶμαι	δηλοῦμαι
τιμᾶσαι	δηλοῖ
τιμᾶται	δηλοῦται
τιμώμεθα	δηλούμεθα
τιμᾶσθε	δηλοῦσθε
τιμῶνται	δηλοῦνται

Present Middle/Passive Imperative

τιμῶ	δηλοῦ
τιμάσθω	δηλούσθω
τιμᾶσθε	δηλοῦσθε
τιμάσθωσαν	δηλούσθωσαν

Present Subjunctive Middle/Passive

τιμῶμαι	δηλῶμαι
τιμᾷ	δηλοῖ
τιμᾶται	δηλῶται
τιμώμεθα	δηλώμεθα
τιμᾶσθε	δηλῶσθε
τιμῶνται	δηλῶνται

Present Middle/Passive Infinitive

τιμᾶσθαι	δηλοῦσθαι

Present Middle/Passive Participle

τιμώμενος, -η, -ον	δηλούμενος, -η, -ον

Imperfect Indicative Middle/Passive	
ἐτιμώμην	ἐδηλούμην
ἐτιμῶ	ἐδηλοῦ
ἐτιμᾶτο	ἐδηλοῦτο
ἐτιμώμεθα	ἐδηλούμεθα
ἐτιμᾶσθε	ἐδηλοῦσθε
ἐτιμῶντο	ἐδηλοῦντο

Exercise

1. καὶ ἠρώτησεν παρ᾿ αὐτῶν ποῦ ὁ Χριστὸς γεννᾶται.
2. οἱ μαθηταὶ ἐφανερουν ταυτα ἃ ἤκουσαν.
3. ὁ δὲ θεος δικαιοι τοὺς υἱοὺς τῶν ἀνθρωπων πιστει καὶ οὐκ ἐργοις.
4. ὁ καυχωμενος ἐν Κυριῳ καυχασθω.
5. καὶ ἦλθον πρὸς τὸν ἱερεα ἱνα ἐρωτησωσιν αὐτον περὶ τῆς συνειδησεως αὐτων.
6. ἐλεγον τὴν ἐξοδον αὐτου ἣν ἠμελλεν πληρουν ἐν Ἱερουσαλημ.
7. ἀκουσας δὲ ὀχλου διαπορευομενου ἐπηρωτησεν τι ἂν εἰη τουτο.
8. πλανασθε μη εἰδοτες τας γραφας μηδε τὴν δυναμιν του θεου.
9. ὠ Πατερ, φανερωσον τὴν δυναμιν σου ἡμιν ἱνα δοξασθη το ὀνομα σου.
10. ἐθεωρουν το ἱερον πεπληρωμενον τῃ δοξῃ του Κυριου.

LESSON **32**

The -μι Verbs: τίθημι

VR.16 In the three common -μι verbs in the New Testament, apart from εἰμί (viz. τίθημι, δίδωμι and ἵστημι) and their compounds, the regular rules of verb accent apply, except:

VR.16.1 the present active subjunctive and the second aorist active subjunctive always have a circumflex accent on the long vowel;

VR.16.2 the present active infinitive has an acute accent on the penult;

VR.16.3 in both the present active participle and the second aorist participle the accent is not recessive.

In the chart of τίθημι which follows, only those forms are included which are likely to provide any difficulty in accentuation. For example, the future θήσω is so entirely regular as not to be worthy of inclusion. For the principal parts and their accents, see p. 148. All of the following accents should be studied in terms of the verb rules in general and *VR.16* in particular.

The second aorist active subjunctive always, according to *VR.16.1*, has a circumflex accent on the long vowel. Because of the shape of the word, that accent *seems* to be recessive (see the following chart). Compound forms of the verb show this is not the case: e.g., the second aorist active subjunctive is ἐπιθῶ, *not* ἐπίθω. By contrast, the second aorist imperative (second person singular) is ἐπίθες, *not* ἐπιθές. But why not ἔπιθες? For this we need:

VR.17 In all verbs compounded with a preposition, the accent of the verb cannot fall farther back than one syllable before the verb proper.

Comment: This limits ἐπιτίθημι in the second aorist active subjunctive (second person singular) from becoming ἔπιθες: the correct accentuation

is ἐπίθες. Yet *VR.17* is broad enough to permit such accents as those in
ἔξεστιν, ὕπαγε, and ἄφες. This rule does not set aside *VR.3*.

Present:			Active		
Indicative	*Subjunctive*	*Participle*		*Imperative*	*Infinitive*
τίθημι	τιθῶ	τιθείς, τιθεῖσα, τιθέν		τίθει	τιθέναι
τίθης	τιθῇς	τιθέντα		τιθέτω	
τίθησιν	τιθῇ			τίθετε	
τίθεμεν	τιθῶμεν			τιθέτωσαν	
τίθετε	τιθῆτε				
τιθέασιν	τιθῶσιν				

Present:			Middle/Passive		
Indicative	*Subjunctive*	*Participle*		*Imperative*	*Infinitive*
τίθεμαι		τιθέμενος, -η, -ον		τίθεσο	τίθεσθαι
etc.				τιθέσθω	
				τιθέσθε	
				τιθέσθωσαν	

Imperfect:	Active	Middle/Passive
	ἐτίθην	ἐτιθέμην
	ἐτίθεις	ἐτίθεσο
	ἐτίθει	ἐτίθετο
	ἐτίθεμεν	ἐτιθέμεθα
	ἐτίθετε	ἐτίθεσθε
	ἐτίθεσαν (or ἐτίθουν)	ἐτίθεντο

Aorist:			First Aorist Active		
Indicative	*Subjunctive*	*Participle*		*Imperative*	*Infinitive*
ἔθηκα					
etc.					

Aorist:

	Second Aorist Active			
Indicative	*Subjunctive*	*Participle*	*Imperative*	*Infinitive*
(use first aorist)	θῶ θῇς θῇ θῶμεν θῆτε θῶσιν	θείς, θεῖσα, θέν θέντα	θές θέτω θέτε θέτωσαν	θεῖναι

Aorist:

	Second Aorist Middle			
ἐθέμην ἔθου ἔθετο ἐθέμεθα ἔθεσθε ἔθεντο	θῶμαι θῇ θῆται θώμεθα θῆσθε θῶνται	θέμενος, -η, -ον	θοῦ θέσθω θέσθε θέσθωσαν	θέσθαι

Exercise

1. καὶ λαβὼν τὸ σωμα ὁ Ἰωσηφ ἔθηκεν αὐτο ἐν τῳ καινῳ μνημειῳ αὐτου.
2. καὶ αὐτος θεις τα γονατα προσηυχετο.
3. καταβησομαι ἵνα θω τας χειρας ἐπ᾽ αὐτην καὶ ζησει.
4. δει ἡμας τιθεναι τον νομον της ἀγαπης ἐν ταις καρδιαις ἡμων καθ᾽ ἡμεραν.
5. πως θωμεν την θυγατερα ἡμων παρα τους ποδας αὐτου;
6. τι ὅτι ἔθου ἐν τῇ καρδιᾳ σου το πραγμα τουτο;
7. καὶ ἐζητουν αὐτον εἰσενεγκειν καὶ θειναι αὐτον ἐνωπιον αὐτου.
8. οὐχ ὑμων ἐστιν γνωναι χρονους ἢ καιρους οὓς ὁ πατηρ ἔθετο ἐν τῇ ἰδιᾳ ἐξουσιᾳ.
9. ὁ ποιμην ὁ καλος την ψυχην αὐτου τιθησιν ὑπερ των προβατων.
10. οἱ ἀποστολοι κατηυλογησαν ἡμας ἐπιτιθεντες τας χειρας ἐφ᾽ ἡμας.

LESSON 33

The -μι Verbs: δίδωμι

The rule framed in the last lesson (viz., *VR.16*) can be applied equally to δίδωμι and to such compounds as ἀποδίδωμι and παραδίδωμι. Most forms which exist only outside the New Testament corpus have been excluded from the following chart.

Present:			Active		
	Indicative	*Subjunctive*	*Participle*	*Imperative*	*Infinitive*
	δίδωμι	διδῶ	διδούς, διδοῦσα, διδόν	δίδου	διδόναι
	δίδως	διδῷς	διδόντα	διδότω	
	δίδωσιν	διδῷ		δίδοτε	
	δίδομεν	διδῶμεν		διδότωσαν	
	δίδοτε	διδῶτε			
	διδόασιν	διδῶσιν			

Present:		Middle/Passive	
	δίδομαι etc.	διδόμενος, -η, -ον	δίδοσθαι

Imperfect:	*Active*	*Middle/Passive*
	ἐδίδουν	ἐδιδόμην
	ἐδίδους	ἐδίδοσο
	ἐδίδου	ἐδίδοτο
	ἐδίδομεν	ἐδιδόμεθα
	ἐδίδοτε	ἐδίδοσθε
	ἐδίδοσαν	ἐδίδοντο

Aorist:	First Aorist Active				
Indicative	*Subjunctive*	*Participle*	*Imperative*	*Infinitive*
ἔδωκα				
etc.				

Aorist:	Second Aorist Active				
(use first	δῶ	δούς, δοῦσα, δόν	δός	δοῦναι
aorist)	δῷς	δόντα	δότω
	δῷ		δότε
	δῶμεν		δότωσαν
	δῶτε		
	δῶσιν		

Aorist:	Second Aorist Middle
ἐδόμην	
ἔδου	
ἔδοτο	
ἐδόμεθα	
ἔδοσθε	
ἔδοντο	

Exercise

1. εἶπε μοι εἰ το χωριον ἀπεδοσθε· ἀποδος μοι, εἰ τι ὀφειλεις.
2. ταυτα παντα σοι δωσω ἐαν πεσων προσκυνησῃς μοι.
3. ὁ δε οὐκ ἤθελεν, ἀλλα ἀπελθων ἐβαλεν αὐτον εἰς φυλακην ἑως ἀποδῳ το ὀφειλομενον.
4. τηρησωμεν τας ἐντολας τας ἡμιν διδομενας.
5. ὁ βασιλευς ἡμιν δεδωκεν ταυτην την πολιν· μη παραδωμεν αὐτην τοις ἐχθροις αὐτου.
6. ἐδοθη μοι πασα ἐξουσια ἐν οὐρανῳ και ἐπι γης.
7. ὁ διδους ἀρτον τοις ἀσθενεσιν ἐξει τον μισθον αὐτου.
8. περιεπατουν δε διδοντες ἱματια τοις λεπροις.
9. δεδωκεισαν δε οἱ ἀρχιερεις ἐντολας.
10. και ὁταν ἀγωσιν ὑμας παραδιδοντες, μη προμεριμνατε τι λαλησητε, ἀλλ᾽ ὁ ἐαν δοθῃ ὑμιν ἐν ἐκεινῃ τῃ ὡρᾳ, τουτο λαλειτε.

The -μι Verbs: ἵστημι

The verb ἵστημι presents peculiar difficulties of inflection, owing to its combination of transitive and intransitive tenses. Be that as it may, both *VR.16* and *VR.17* (cf. Lesson 32) still hold true, both for ἵστημι and for its several compounds.

This verbs has *two* aorist participles, a first and a second; and *neither* has a recessive accent. This is an extension, rather than an abrogation, of *VR.16.3*.

Present:	Active				
	Indicative	*Subjunctive*	*Participle*	*Imperative*	*Infinitive*
	ἵστημι	ἱστῶ	ἱστάς, ἱστᾶσα, ἱστάν	ἵστη	ἱστάναι
	ἵστης	ἱστῇς	ἱστάντα	ἱστάτω	
	ἵστησιν	ἱστῇ		ἵστατε	
	ἵσταμεν	ἱστῶμεν		ἱστάτωσαν	
	ἵστατε	ἱστῆτε			
	ἱστᾶσιν[1]	ἱστῶσιν			

Present:	Middle and Passive				
	Indicative	*Subjunctive*	*Participle*	*Imperative*	*Infinitive*
	ἵσταμαι		ἱστάμενος, -η, -ον	ἵστασο	ἵστασθαι
	etc.			ἱστάσθω	
				ἵστασθε	
				ἱστάσθωσαν	

1. This is not an irregular accent, because the ending is -ασιν: i.e., ἱστά+ασιν → ἱστᾶσιν.

Imperfect:	Active	Middle/Passive
	ἵστην	ἱστάμην
	ἵστης	ἵστασο
	ἵστη	ἵστατο
	ἵσταμεν	ἱστάμεθα
	ἵστατε	ἵστασθε
	ἵστασαν	ἵσταντο

Aorist:

First Aorist Active

Indicative	Subjunctive	Participle	Imperative	Infinitive
ἔστησα	στήσω	στήσας, στήσασα, στῆσαν	στῆσον	στῆσαι
ἔστησας	στήσῃς		στησάτω	
ἔστησεν	στήσῃ		στήσατε	
ἐστήσαμεν	στήσωμεν		στησάτωσαν	
ἐστήσατε	στήσητε			
ἔστησαν	στήσωσιν			

Aorist:

Second Aorist Active

Indicative	Subjunctive	Participle	Imperative	Infinitive
ἔστην	στῶ	στάς, στᾶσα, στάν	στῆθι	στῆναι
ἔστης	στῇς	στάντα	στήτω	
ἔστη	στῇ		στῆτε	
ἔστημεν	στῶμεν		στήτωσαν	
ἔστητε	στῆτε			
ἔστησαν	στῶσιν			

The verb ἵστημι has two perfect participles; but both conform to the accent rules already established: first perfect participle, ἑστηκώς, ἑστηκυῖα, ἑστηκός; and second aorist participle, ἑστώς, ἑστῶσα, ἑστός.

Exercise

1. ταυτα δε αὐτων λαλουντων αὐτος ἐστη ἐν μεσῳ αὐτων.
2. τα νυν παραγγελλει ὁ θεος τοις ἀνθρωποις παντας πανταχου μετανοειν, καθ᾽ ὅτι ἐστησεν ἡμεραν ἐν ᾗ μελλει κρινειν την οἰκουμενην ἐν δικαιοσυνῃ.
3. ὁ δε Ἰησους ἐσταθη ἐμπροσθεν του ἡγεμονος.
4. δει οὖν τον Παυλον στηναι ἐν τῳ συνεδριῳ.

5. ἐβλεψαν συν αὐτοις ἑστωτα τον ἀνθρωπον τον τεθεραπευμενον.

6. ἀνθρωπε, τις με κατεστησεν κριτην ἐφ᾽ ὑμας;

7. ἡ μητηρ και οἱ ἀδελφοι αὐτου εἱστηκεισαν ἐξω ζητουντες αὐτῳ λαλησαι.

8. δους δε αὐτῃ την χειρα ἀνεστησεν αὐτην.

9. πορευεσθε και σταθεντες λαλειτε ἐν τῳ ἱερῳ παντα το ῥηματα της ζωης ταυτης.

10. εἰ τις πιστευει εἰς ἐμε ἀναστησω αὐτον ἐν τῃ ἐσχατῃ ἡμερᾳ.

Other -μι Verbs

There are several other -μι verbs in the New Testament, in addition to the three that have taken up the last three lessons. Detailed treatment of their accents would require disproportionate energy; but the following observations enable the student to accent most forms of -μι verbs correctly:

1. The verb εἰμί is in a class of its own. Most of its forms have been treated elsewhere in this *Manual*, and need not be repeated. Not yet mentioned are the accents on the imperative of this verb:

> ἴσθι
> ἔστω
> ἔστε
> ἔστωσαν

2. Verbs ending in -υμι, like δείκνυμι, follow the accent pattern of τίθημι *as long as they behave like -μι verbs*. In the New Testament, however, there is a tendency for -υμι verbs to assimilate themselves to -ω verbs: e.g., δεικνύω. When such assimilation occurs, the rules for accenting verbs in the -ω system prevail.

3. Two common -μι verbs in the New Testament are ἀφίημι and συνίημι, both based on a simpler verb which is not found by itself in the New Testament: viz., ἵημι. In general ἵημι is accented like τίθημι. See the accented list on p. 148 for the principal parts of ἀφίημι: these should be carefully memorized.

4. The verb φημί is found in only four forms in the New Testament. Three of these are in the present tense, and are enclitics: φημί, φησίν, and φασίν. Note that φησίν, the third person singular form, is an ordinary disyllabic enclitic: it does *not* adopt the special rules which apply to another third person singular disyllabic enclitic, ἐστίν (cf. *EPR.8*). The fourth form of this verb, ἔφη, is not an enclitic; it follows the basic recessive rule for verbs (*VR.1*).

5. Particular -μι verbs not mentioned here normally present no problem with their accents, once the student is thoroughly familiar with the material of the last four lessons.

Exercise

1. ὁ δε φησιν Πασα ἁμαρτια και βλασφημια ἀφεθησεται τοις ἀνθρωποις.
2. οὐκ εἰπομεν καθως φασιν τινες ἡμας λεγειν.
3. και ἀφες ἡμιν τα ὀφειληματα ἡμων, ὡς και ἡμεις ἀφηκαμεν τοις ὀφειλεταις ἡμων.
4. ὁ δε ἐφη Κυριε, σωσον, ἀπολλυμεθα.
5. ὁ δε φησιν σοι Ἀφεωνται αἱ ἁμαρτιαι αὐτης αἱ πολλαι.
6. ἐν δε παραβολαις τα παντα γινεται μηποτε ἐπιστρεψωσιν και ἀφεθῃ αὐτοις.
7. τοτε δεικνυσιν αὐτῳ ὁ διαβολος πασας τας βασιλειας του κοσμου.
8. και ὁπου ἀν εἰσεπορευετο ἐν ταις ἀγοραις ἐτιθεσαν τους ἀσθενουντας.
9. ἐκεινοις δε τοις ἐξω ἐν παραβολαις τα παντα γινεται, ἱνα ἀκουοντες ἀκουωσιν και μη συνιωσιν.
10. παντες γαρ οἱ λαβοντες μαχαιραν ἐν μαχαιρῃ ἀπολουνται.

Some New Testament Passages

Below are several New Testament passages with all accents omitted. At this stage the student should be able not only to insert the accents correctly, but to explain why each accent is chosen and why it is placed on that syllable. If a particular word is not known, it may be checked in a lexicon; but a copy of the New Testament should not be consulted until every effort has been made to insert all accents correctly.

Matthew 5:3 μακαριοι οἱ πτωχοι τῳ πνευματι, ὁτι αὑτων ἐστιν ἡ βασιλεια των οὑρανων.

Matthew 16:21 ἀπο τοτε ἠρξατο ὁ Ἰησους δεικνυειν τοις μαθηταις αὑτου ὁτι δει αὑτον εἰς Ἱεροσολυμα ἀπελθειν και πολλα παθειν ἀπο των πρεσβυτερων και ἀρχιερεων και γραμματεων και ἀποκτανθηναι και τῃ τριτῃ ἡμερᾳ ἐγερθηναι.

Mark 12:28 και προσελθων εἰς των γραμματεων ἀκουσας αὑτων συζητουν-των, ἰδων ὁτι καλως ἀπεκριθη αὑτοις, ἐπηρωτησεν αὑτον, Ποια ἐστιν ἐντολη πρωτη παντων;

John 7:29-30 ἐγω οἰδα αὑτον, ὁτι παρ᾽ αὑτου εἰμι κἀκεινος με ἀπεστειλεν. ἐζητουν οὐν αὑτον πιασαι, και οὐδεις ἐπεβαλεν ἐπ᾽ αὑτον την χειρα, ὁτι οὐπω ἐληλυθει ἡ ὡρα αὑτου.

John 9:40-41 ἠκουσαν ἐκ των Φαρισαιων ταυτα οἱ μετ᾽ αὑτου ὁντες, και εἰπον αὑτῳ, Μη και ἡμεις τυφλοι ἐσμεν; εἰπεν αὑτοις ὁ Ἰησους, Εἰ τυφλοι ἠτε, οὐκ ἀν εἰχετε ἁμαρτιαν· νυν δε λεγετε ὁτι Βλεπομεν· ἡ ἁμαρτια ὑμων μενει.

Acts 9:5-6 εἰπεν δε, Τις εἰ, κυριε; ὁ δε, Ἐγω εἰμι Ἰησους ὁν συ διωκεις· ἀλλα ἀναστηθι και εἰσελθε εἰς την πολιν, και λαληθησεται σοι ὁ τι σε δει ποιειν.

Acts 25:5 οἱ οὐν ἐν ὑμιν, φησιν, δυνατοι συγκαταβαντες εἰ τι ἐστιν ἐν τῳ ἀνδρι ἀτοπον κατηγορειτωσαν αὑτου.

Acts 27:23–24a παρεστη γαρ μοι ταυτη τη νυκτι του θεου οὐ εἰμι ἐγω, ᾧ καὶ λατρευω, ἀγγελος λεγων, *Μη φοβου, Παυλε.*

Romans 15:13 ὁ δε θεος της ἐλπιδος πληρωσαι ὑμας πασης χαρας και εἰρηνης ἐν τῳ πιστευειν, εἰς το περισσευειν ὑμας ἐν τῃ ἐλπιδι ἐν δυναμει πνευματος ἁγιου.

Galatians 1:6–7 θαυμαζω ὁτι οὑτως ταχεως μετατιθεσθε ἀπο του καλεσαντος ὑμας ἐν χαριτι Χριστου εἰς ἑτερον εὑαγγελιον, ὁ οὑκ ἐστιν ἀλλο· εἰ μη τινες εἰσιν οἱ ταρασσοντες ὑμας και θελοντες μεταστρεψαι το εὑαγγελιον του Χριστου.

Galatians 6:3 εἰ γαρ δοκει τις εἰναι τι μηδεν ὠν, φρεναπατᾳ ἑαυτον.

LESSON 37

The Next Steps

The rules of accentuation explained, illustrated and practiced in the preceding pages are enough (some would say more than enough!) for the average reader of the Greek New Testament. But some might wish to go on, or at least have the way ahead pointed out for future exploration. Serious students will want to consult the large grammars and specialized philological studies in the area; but perhaps a few brief paragraphs outlining the directions such study might take would not be without usefulness.

1. This *Manual* has consistently spoken of the 'rules' of accentuation; but the caution advanced in the Preface needs to be reiterated. These 'rules' are neither arbitrary decrees manufactured by dusty grammarians, nor something akin to scientific laws bound up with the very nature of physical reality. Rather, they are the deductions of grammarians who seek to formulate in 'rules' the patterns of the language being studied. This *Manual* formulates more rules than most treatments of Greek accents, partly because it is a little more comprehensive and partly because rules have been formulated in a pedagogically convenient pattern (e.g., *VR.2* and *VR.9* could have been linked together, but not conveniently in this *Manual*); but it does not *impose* anything new. Most of its rules are well known; and, even where not known in these precise statements, readers of Greek who already know where the accents go but who have not formulted as many rules, will see some new formulation and say, 'Of course. That's what I've been doing. It's nice to see proper practice reduced to memorizable formulations.' *Mutatis mutandis*, more formulations could be offered, some known, some new, to cover a widening circle of exceptional forms. The study of advanced morphology, for instance, would lead the student to 'discover' some 'new' rules. But the point is that the grammarian's task is essentially one of classification and formulation, prompted perhaps by sheer curiosity, by pedagogical concerns, or by the desire to understand a little better some literary corpus.

Further study of the Greek New Testament at this stage in a student's career can proceed along a broader front than would be the case if the 'rules' of accents were unknown. But it must not proceed as if rules of grammar, including accent rules, are always like the laws 'of the Medes and the Persians which cannot be altered'. Rather, they constitute a framework for further explorations into the organization and genius of the language.

2. The accents in the New Testament differ to some extent from those of earlier Attic Greek. Attic Greek insists on ὁμοῖος, θλίψις and ἐρῆμος; the Greek of the New Testament, on ὅμοιος, θλῖψις and ἔρημος. Long lists of such changes, and some explanations, are offered by the large grammars and lexica. But some ambivalence persists into the New Testament period, and it takes some experience to spot such details. Editors of printed Greek Testaments tend today to standardize some of the accent variations they find in the manuscripts. David Holly, *A Complete Categorized Greek–English New Testament Vocabulary* (Grand Rapids: Baker, 1978), pp. 116–18, provides a list of differences in accent and orthography between the Bauer-Arndt-Gingrich *Lexicon* and the Moulton-Geden *Concordance*.

3. Heteroclites (words which have forms belonging to two or more different declensional paradigms) sometimes offer problems not only in inflection, but in accentuation; and these are worth exploring.

4. We have already noted several pairs of words distinguished only by accent. Not a few exegetical questions turn on such pairs. Compare ἀλλά and ἄλλα: which should we read in John 6:23? Does Hebrews 9:2 require ἅγια or ἁγία? Are we to prefer ἄρα or ἆρα in Galatians 2:17? Should we adopt κρινοῦσιν or κρίνουσιν in I Corinthians 6:2? There is a substantial number of such exegetical problems in the New Testament, all worthy of detailed study. In addition to such exegetical problems, the study of cognates often turns up a wealth of detail, some of it invaluable for the study of accents. If we extend our borders beyond the New Testament, many more and interesting cognates may be included: e.g., the word ἀποστόλος (paroxytone), which is found in Demosthenes, where it means 'naval expedition'.

5. A most interesting area of study is the accentuation on Greek proper names, which cannot always be brought under the normal rules. The grammarian A. T. Robertson pointed out a long time ago that 'in Greek, as in English, men claim the right to accent their own names as they will.' The accent is one of the factors in the old debate about whether Nympha (or Nymphas) in Colossians 4:15 is a man or a woman. See also the problem in Romans 16:7. Still more difficult is the study of the accentuation of foreign transliterated loan words, including proper names. Is Caiaphas ὁ Καϊάφας or ὁ Καϊαφᾶς? On what basis are such decisions made?

6. As long as Greek accents reflected pitch and not stress, then long vowels could easily be stressed even when some other syllable received the

acute accent. As accents began to reflect stress and not pitch, however, then the stress which at one time was placed on a long vowel might be placed on the accented syllable *at the expense of the long vowel.* For instance the long η in Attic Greek's ἀνάθημα might be easy to preserve as long as the η was stressed; but if the accented α was *stressed* (as opposed to receiving a rising pitch), it was difficult to preserve the long η. Soon pronunciation, and then spelling, became ἀνάθεμα. Similarly the distinction between ἔχωμεν and ἔχομεν, if transmitted orally, might very easily evaporate.

It must be admitted that the significance for accents of this sort of phenomenon, adduced by older grammarians, is disputed by some modern philologists, who think that accents reflected pitch, not stress, throughout the New Testament period. Their cautions and helpful controls are laudatory; but one suspects that the process of changing from a pitch accent to a stress accent did not take place overnight. If two centuries or more were necessary for the complete change to take place, then perhaps we are not remiss in seeing some signs of the change reflected in some non-Attic spellings in the New Testament. At any rate, a great deal of work has been done in this area, and is worth probing by the student whose curiosity has been whetted.

Some Accented Principal Parts

The following chart provides accented principal parts of the most common irregular verbs in the New Testament. Virtually all of these forms follow the recessive rule (*VR.1*),[1] and so in principle the student should be able to insert the accents himself; but they are provided for convenience.

A dash stands in place of a form where the form is not found in the New Testament. A few forms occur only in compounds (e.g., the parts of βαίνω); but because accentuation is reckoned from the end of a word, there is no point in drawing attention to such forms in the following chart.

Present	Future	Aorist Active	Perfect Active	Perfect Passive	Aorist Passive
Paradigm Verb					
λύω	λύσω	ἔλυσα	λέλυκα	λέλυμαι	ἐλύθην
Paradigm Contract Verbs					
φιλέω	φιλήσω	ἐφίλησα	πεφίληκα	πεφίλημαι	ἐφιλήθην
τιμάω	τιμήσω	ἐτίμησα	τετίμηκα	τετίμημαι	ἐτιμήθην
φανερόω	φανερώσω	ἐφανέρωσα	πεφανέρωκα	πεφανέρωμαι	ἐφανερώθην
Aspirated Perfect (χ instead of κ) Verbs					
κηρύσσω	κηρύξω	ἐκήρυξα	—	κεκήρυγμαι	ἐκηρύχθην
πράσσω	πράξω	ἔπραξα	πέπραχα	πέπραγμαι	—

---

1. The only exception is the future of verbs with liquid stems; and this exception is more apparent than real (cf. Lesson 18).

Irregular Verbs

ἀγγέλω	ἀγγελῶ	ἤγγειλα	ἤγγελκα	ἤγγελμαι	ἠγγέλην
ἄγω	ἄξω	ἤγαγον	—	ἦγμαι	ἤχθην
αἱρέω	αἱρήσομαι	εἷλον	—	ᾕρημαι	ᾑρέθην
αἴρω	ἀρῶ	ἦρα	ἦρκα	ἦρμαι	ἤρθην
ἀκούω	ἀκούσω or ἀκούσομαι	ἤκουσα	ἀκήκοα	—	ἠκούσθην
ἁμαρτάνω	ἁμαρτήσω	ἥμαρτον or ἡμάρτησα	ἡμάρτηκα	—	—
ἀνοίγω	ἀνοίξω	ἤνοιξα	ἀνέῳγα	ἀνέῳγμαι	ἠνοίχθην
ἀποθνῄσκω	ἀποθανοῦμαι	ἀπέθανον	τέθνηκα	—	—
ἀποκτείνω	ἀποκτενῶ	ἀπέκτεινα	—	—	ἀπεκτάνθην
ἀρέσκω	ἀρέσω	ἤρεσα	—	—	—
ἀρνέομαι	ἀρνήσομαι	ἠρνησάμην	—	ἤρνημαι	ἠρνήθην
βαίνω	βήσομαι	ἔβην	βέβηκα	—	—
βάλλω	βαλῶ	ἔβαλον	βέβληκα	βέβλημαι	ἐβλήθην
γαμέω	γαμήσω	ἔγημα	γεγάμηκα	—	ἐγαμήθην
γίνομαι	γενήσομαι	ἐγενόμην	γέγονα	γεγένημαι	ἐγενήθην
γινώσκω	γνώσομαι	ἔγνων	ἔγνωκα	ἔγνωσμαι	ἐγνώσθην
γράφω	γράψω	ἔγραψα	γέγραφα	γέγραμμαι	ἐγράφην
δέχομαι	δέξομαι	ἐδεξάμην	—	δέδεγμαι	ἐδέχθην
διδάσκω	διδάξω	ἐδίδαξα	—	—	ἐδιδάχθην
διώκω	διώξω	ἐδίωξα	—	δεδίωγμαι	ἐδιώχθην
δύναμαι	δυνήσομαι	ἐδυνάμην or ἠδυνάμην	—	—	ἠδυνήθην or ἠδυνάσθην
ἐγγίζω	ἐγγίσω or ἐγγιῶ	ἤγγισα	ἤγγικα	—	—
ἐγείρω	ἐγερῶ	ἤγειρα	—	ἐγήγερμαι	ἠγέρθην
ἐλπίζω	ἐλπίσω or ἐλπιῶ	ἤλπισα	ἤλπικα	—	—
ἐργάζομαι	—	ἠργασάμην	—	εἴργασμαι	εἰργάσθην
εὑρίσκω	εὑρήσω	εὗρον	εὕρηκα	—	εὑρέθην
εὔχομαι	εὔξομαι	εὐξάμην	—	—	—
θέλω	θελήσω	ἠθέλησα	—	—	—
καίω	καύσω	ἔκαυσα	—	κέκαυμαι	ἐκαύθην
καλέω	καλέσω	ἐκάλεσα	κέκληκα	κέκλημαι	ἐκλήθην
κλίνω	κλινῶ	ἔκλινα	κέκλικα	—	ἐκλίθην
κράζω	κράξω	ἔκραξα	κέκραγα	—	—
κρίνω	κρινῶ	ἔκρινα	κέκρικα	κέκριμαι	ἐκρίθην
λαμβάνω	λήμψομαι	ἔλαβον	εἴληφα	εἴλημμαι	ἐλήμφθην
λείπω	λείψω	ἔλιπον	λέλοιπα	λέλειμμαι	ἐλείφην
μανθάνω	—	ἔμαθον	μεμάθηκα	—	—
μέλλω	μελλήσω	ἤμελλον or ἔμελλον	—	—	—
μένω	μενῶ	ἔμεινα	μεμένηκα	—	—
μιμνῄσκω	μνήσω	ἔμνησα	—	μέμνημαι	ἐμνήσθην
πάσχω	—	ἔπαθον	πέπονθα	—	—
πείθω	πείσω	ἔπεισα	πέποιθα	πέπεισμαι	ἐπείσθην
πίνω	πίομαι	ἔπιον	πέπωκα	—	ἐπόθην
πίπτω	πεσοῦμαι	ἔπεσον	πέπτωκα	—	—
σπείρω	—	ἔσπειρα	—	ἔσπαρμαι	ἐσπάρην

Irregular Verbs (continued)

στέλλω	στελῶ	ἔστειλα	ἔσταλκα	ἔσταλμαι	ἐστάλην
στρέφω	στρέψω	ἔστρεψα	—	ἔστραμμαι	ἐστράφην
σώζω	σώσω	ἔσωσα	σέσωκα	σέσωσμαι	ἐσώθην
τελέω	τελέσω	ἐτέλεσα	τετέλεκα	τετέλεσμαι	ἐτελέσθην
τρέχω	—	ἔδραμον	—	—	—
φαίνω	φανοῦμαι	ἔφανα	—	—	ἐφάνην
φεύγω	φεύξομαι	ἔφυγον	πέφευγα	—	—
φθείρω	φθερῶ	ἔφθειρα	—	ἔφθαρμαι	ἐφθάρην

Irregular Verbs Derived from More than One Verb

ἔρχομαι	ἐλεύσομαι	ἦλθον	ἐλήλυθα	—	—
ἐσθίω	φάγομαι	ἔφαγον	—	—	—
ἔχω	ἕξω	ἔσχον	ἔσχηκα	—	—
λέγω	ἐρῶ	εἶπον	εἴρηκα	εἴρημαι	ἐρρήθην or ἐρρέθην
ὁράω	ὄψομαι	εἶδον	ἑώρακα or ἑόρακα	—	ὤφθην
φέρω	οἴσω	ἤνεγκον	ἐνήνοχα	—	ἠνέχθην

Paradigm -μι Verbs

τίθημι	θήσω	ἔθηκα	τέθεικα	τέθειμαι	ἐτέθην
δίδωμι	δώσω	ἔδωκα	δέδωκα	δέδομαι	ἐδόθην
ἵστημι	στήσω	ἔστησα			
		ἔστην	ἔστηκα	—	ἐστάθην

Other -μι Verbs

ἀπόλλυμι	ἀπολέσω or ἀπολῶ	ἀπώλεσα	—	—	—
ἀπόλλυμαι	ἀπολοῦμαι	ἀπωλόμην	ἀπόλωλα	—	—
ἀφίημι	ἀφήσω	ἄφηκα	—	ἀφέωμαι	ἀφέθην
δείκνυμι	δείξω	ἔδειξα	—	δέδειγμαι	ἐδείχθην
εἰμί	ἔσομαι	ἤμην (impf.)	—		

Summary of Accent Rules

General Rules of Accent

GR.1 Apart from specific exceptions later to be enumerated, every Greek word must have an accent, but only one accent.

GR.2 An acute accent may stand only on an ultima, a penult, or an antepenult; a circumflex accent may stand only on an ultima or a penult; and a grave accent may stand only on an ultima.

GR.3 The circumflex accent cannot stand on a short syllable.

GR.4 If the ultima is long, then:

> **GR.4.1** the antepenult cannot have any accent, and
>
> **GR.4.2** the penult, if it is accented at all, must have the acute.

GR.5 If the ultima is short, then a long penult, if it is accented at all, must have the circumflex accent.

GR.6 An acute accent on the ultima of a word is changed to a grave when followed, without intervening mark of punctuation, by another word or words.

Verb Rules of Accent

VR.1 The accent in finite verbal forms is recessive.

VR.2 In contract verbs, if either of the contracting syllables, before contraction, has an accent, then the resulting contracted syllable has an accent.

> **VR.2.1** If the resulting contracted syllable is a penult or an antepenult, and has an accent, the General Rules always tell what kind of accent it will be.

VR.2.2 If the resulting contracted syllable is an ultima, and has an accent, the accent must be a circumflex.

VR.3 In compound verbs, the accent cannot go farther back than the augment.

VR.4 The present infinitive in all voices has a recessive accent.

VR.5 Whenever *a* is found in the ultima of first aorist active forms or of perfect active forms, it is always short.

VR.6 The first aorist infinitive active is accented on the penult.

VR.7 For purposes of order, all second aorist active imperatives should be made to follow *VR.1* (the recessive rule), *except* the second person singular of the second aorist imperative of the forms corresponding to λέγω and ἔρχομαι (but not their compounds). This exception holds true regardless of whether such forms are pure second aorist or mixed second and first aorist.

VR.8 The second aorist active infinitive has a circumflex accent on the ultima.

VR.9 In the future tense, active or middle voice, liquid verbs have the same accents as do -εω verbs in the present tense, active or middle voice.

VR.10 The second aorist imperative middle second person singular has a circumflex accent on the ultima; and the second aorist infinitive middle has an accent on the penult.

VR.11 Both the perfect active infinitive and the perfect middle/passive infinitive have an acute accent on the penult.

VR.12 The aorist passive infinitive has a circumflex accent on the penult.

VR.13 In the subjunctive mood, all accents adhere to *VR.1* (the recessive rule) except the first aorist passive and the second aorist passive.

VR.14 In -αω contract verbs, if the contracted syllable centers on an *a* or an *ą*, that syllable is long.

VR.15 In -οω contract verbs, *VR.2.2* overrides the exception which says the diphthongs *αι* and *οι* are short when final.

VR.16 In the three common -μι verbs in the New Testament, apart from εἰμί (viz. τίθημι, δίδωμι and ἵστημι) and their compounds, the regular rules of verb accent apply, except:

VR.16.1 the present active subjunctive and the second aorist active subjunctive always have a circumflex accent on the long vowel;

VR.16.2 the present active infinitive has an acute accent on the penult;

VR.16.3 in both the present active participle and the second aorist participle the accent is not recessive.

VR.17 In all verbs compounded with a preposition, the accent of the verb cannot fall farther back than one syllable before the verb proper.

Noun Rules of Accent

NR.1 In nouns, the accent remains on the same syllable as in the nominative singular, as nearly as the General Rules and certain specific exceptions (*NR.5* and *NR.11*) will permit.

NR.2 In both the first and second declensions, when the ultima takes an acute accent in the nominative singular, it has the circumflex accent in the genitives and datives of both numbers, and elsewhere the acute accent.

NR.3 In both the first and second declensions, when the ultima in the nominative singular has a circumflex accent, the circumflex accent remains on the ultima in all the singular forms.

NR.4 The *a* in the ultima of nominative and accusative plural neuter nouns is always considered short.

NR.5 In the first declension only, the genitive plural exhibits an exception to the basic noun rule (*NR.1*): the genitive plural *must* have a circumflex accent on the ultima regardless of where the accent falls in the nominative singular.

NR.6 The *a* in the ultima of all first declension accusative plural nouns is always considered long.

NR.7 In first declension nouns ending in *a*, or *aς*, whether the *a* in the ultima is long or short in the nominative singular, it is the same in the vocative and the accusative singular.

NR.8 The *a* in the ultima of first declension feminine nouns is considered long when it occurs in the singular genitive and dative.

NR.9 The final *a* in the vocative of first declension masculine nouns is considered short, unless there is a long -*aς* ultima in the nominative singular, in which instance it is long.

NR.10 Whenever an *a* occurs in the final syllable of accusative singular or accusative plural forms of third declension nouns, that *a* is short.

NR.11 Monosyllabic nouns of the third declension normally accent the ultima in the genitive and dative of both numbers. In the genitive plural, that accent must be circumflex; elsewhere, acute.

NR.12 Third declension nouns whose stems end in -*αντ*, and whose dative plural therefore has a penult which could be long or short, will always reckon that syllable long if it has an accent.

NR.13 Third declension neuter nouns of the second (-*ες*) type adhere, in all inflections except the nominative/accusative singular, to *VR.2* (including *VR.2.1* and *VR.2.2*).

NR.14 Nouns ending with -*ις* in the nominative singular and -*εως* in the genitive singular constitute a major exception to the rule that if the ultima is long the antepenult cannot be accented (*GR.4.1*); and this only in the genitive singular and plural.

Indeclinable Word Rules of Accent

IWR.1 The accents on indeclinable words adhere to the General Rules, but must be learned by inspection.

IWR.2 In elision, oxytone prepositions and conjunctions lose their accent.

IWR.3 Adverbs whose spelling is identical with a neuter accusative form of the corresponding adjective adopt the same accent as that of the borrowed form.

IWR.4 Adverbs generated by replacing the final ν of the genitive plural of an adjective with a ς retain the accent of the genitive plural adjective.

Adjective Rules of Accent

AR.1 Second and first declension adjectives adopt accent patterns like those laid down for nouns in *NR.1, NR.2, NR.4* and *NR.6*.

AR.2 Second and first declension adjectives with stems ending in a vowel or ρ (and which therefore have an *a* suffix in the feminine singular of all cases) construe the *a* in the ultima of all feminine singular forms as long.

AR.3 Third declension adjectives adopt accent patterns like those laid down for nouns in *NR.1, NR.4* and *NR.10*.

AR.4 Third declension adjectives of the second (-ες) type adhere, in all inflections except the nominative masculine/feminine singular, to *VR.2* (including *VR.2.1* and *VR.2.2*).

AR.5 Mixed third and first declension adjectives normally adhere to *AR.3*, and also to the accent patterns of *NR.11* and *NR.12*, in the masculine and neuter genders; but they follow the accent pattern of first declension *nouns* (not adjectives!) in the feminine gender.

AR.6 Those comparative and superlative adjectives which are formed by substituting -τερος and -τατος respectively for the final ς of the nominative masculine singular form of second and first declension adjectives follow *AR.1* and *AR.2*.

AR.7 All second aorist active participles have the same accents as the corresponding form of the present participle of εἰμί.

AR.8 In the present middle/passive, the first aorist middle, the second aorist middle, and the present of the irregular verb δύναμαι, the accent on the participle is recessive; but in the perfect middle/passive, the accent of the participle is always on the penult.

Enclitic and Proclitic Rules of Accent

EPR.1 The word before an enclitic does not change an acute accent on the ultima to a grave accent.

EPR.2 If the word preceding an enclitic has an acute accent on the antepenult, or a circumflex accent on the penult, then there is an additional accent, an acute, on the ultima.

EPR.3 If the word preceding an enclitic has an acute on the penult, then:

EPR.3.1 a disyllabic enclitic retains its accent;

EPR.3.2 a monosyllabic enclitic loses its accent.

EPR.4 If the word preceding an enclitic has a circumflex accent on the ultima, then both monosyllabic and disyllabic enclitics normally lose their accent.

EPR.5 If the word before an enclitic is itself a proclitic (except *οὐ, οὐκ* or *οὐχ*) or an enclitic, it has an acute accent on the ultima.

EPR.6 An enclitic retains its accent when:

EPR.6.1 there is emphasis on the enclitic;

EPR.6.2 the enclitic stands at the head of its clause;

EPR.6.3 the enclitic is preceded by *οὐ, οὐκ,* or *οὐχ,* as a separate word.

EPR.7 When a proclitic stands alone or at the end of a clause, it is then accented.

EPR.8 The verbal form *ἐστίν* becomes *ἔστιν,* completely losing its character as an enclitic:

EPR.8.1 when it stands at the beginning of a sentence or clause;

EPR.8.2 when signifying existence or possibility;

EPR.8.3 when it is preceded by *οὐκ, μή, ὡς, εἰ, καί, ἀλλά* (or *ἀλλ'*), *τοῦτο* (when elided as *τοῦτ'*).

EPR.8.4 when it is strongly emphatic.

EPR.9 When an enclitic forms the last part of a compound word, the compound is accented as if the enclitic were a separate word.

Pronoun Rules of Accent

PR.1 Unless otherwise specified, pronouns follow the accent patterns laid down in *AR.1.*

PR.2 The interrogative pronoun *τίς* in all its declensional forms *always* has an acute accent on the first syllable; and the indefinite pronoun *τις* is an enclitic.

PR.3 The indefinite relative pronoun *ὅστις* follows the basic noun rule *NR.1,* but also *EPR.9.*

Key to the Exercises

Lesson 2

1. ἀποστολὸς   Two accents (*GR.1*); location of the acute (*GR.2*); circumflex on a short syllable (*GR.3*).

   ἀποστολος   See *GR.2*; *GR.3*.
   Χρῖστου   See *GR.3*; *GR.4.2*.
   Ἰῆσους   See *GR.4.2*.
   θὲου   See *GR.2*; *GR.4.2*.
   πρὼτος   See *GR.5*.
   ὁ υἱός τοῦ ἄνθρωπου   υἱός: See *GR.6*; ἄνθρωπου; See *GR.4.1*.
   ἀνθρῶπῳ   See *GR.4.2*.

2. δίκαιος   Exclude δικαίος because of *GR.5*.
   ἀνθρώποις   Exclude ἄνθρωποις because of *GR.4.1*.
   δούλῳ   Exclude δοῦλῳ because of *GR.4.2*.
   αὐτῷ   Exclude αὐτῳ because of *GR.4.2*.
   σκοτίᾳ   Exclude σκοτία because of *GR.2*.

Lesson 3

1. λαμβάνετε
2. ἐγείρω
3. ἔχεις
4. θεραπεύουσιν
5. μένει
6. πέμπουσιν
7. κρίνετε
8. ἐσθίεις
9. εὑρίσκομεν
10. σώζει

Lesson 4

1. λαλοῦμεν
2. ποιοῦσιν
3. θεραπεύει
4. καλεῖς
5. μισῶ
6. αἰτεῖ
7. ζητεῖτε
8. φιλοῦμεν
9. μαρτυροῦσιν
10. τηρεῖ

Lesson 5

Exercise A:

1. ἀπόστολος θεραπεύει παραλυτικόν;
2. Χριστὸς κρίνει ἀνθρώπους καὶ ἀγγέλους.
3. μαρτυροῦμεν καὶ λαὸς μετανοεῖ.
4. ὦ Ἰσραήλ, θάνατον ζητεῖτε;
5. ἀπόστολοι λαλοῦσιν καὶ διάκονοι ἔχουσιν φόβον.
6. φόβος λαμβάνει ἀδελφοὺς καὶ λαόν.
7. ἀδελφὸς ἔχει ἀγρόν.
8. κύριοι πέμπουσιν ἀγγέλους καὶ λόγους γράφουσιν.
9. Ἰουδαῖοι καὶ Φαρισαῖοι αἰτοῦσιν φίλους.
10. μισεῖ κόσμον καὶ ζητεῖ φίλον.

Exercise B:

1. οἱ δοῦλοι ποιοῦσιν ὁδὸν τῷ κυρίῳ.
2. μετανοοῦσιν καὶ μισοῦσιν πειρασμόν.
3. ὁ Ἰησοῦς εὐλογεῖ τὸν ἄρτον καὶ τὸν οἶνον τοῦ ἐχθροῦ.
4. ἄνθρωπος καὶ διάκονος λαμβάνουσιν τὸν καρπὸν τοῦ πρεσβυτέρου.
5. ὁ ἥλιος καὶ ὁ ἄνεμος θεραπεύουσιν.
6. ὁ υἱὸς τοῦ θεοῦ ζητεῖ τοὺς οὐρανούς;
7. παρθένοι γινώσκουσιν τοὺς λόγους τοῦ ὄχλου.
8. ὁ ἄγγελος γράφει νόμους τῷ κόσμῳ.
9. ὁ διάβολος μισεῖ τὸν τοῦ θεοῦ ναόν.
10. ὁ Κύριος σῴζει ἁμαρτωλούς.

Lesson 6

Exercise A:

1. οἱ ἀπόστολοι λαλοῦσιν τὸ εὐαγγέλιον κυρίοις καὶ δούλοις.
2. τὰ τέκνα αἰτεῖ τοὺς πρεσβυτέρους ἱμάτια.
3. ἄγγελοι θεωροῦσιν τὸ πρόσωπον τοῦ θεοῦ.
4. οἱ ἄνθρωποι ἔχουσιν πρόβατα καὶ πλοῖον.

5. βλέπομεν τὰ σημεῖα τῶν καιρῶν.
6. τὸ σάββατον τοῦ θεοῦ σημεῖόν ἐστίν.
7. Χριστὸς εὐλογεῖ τὸ ποτήριον οἴνου καὶ τὸν ἄρτον.
8. οἱ διάκονοι τηροῦσιν τὰ ποτήρια τοῦ ἱεροῦ Ἱεροσολύμων.
9. τὰ δαιμόνια φιλεῖ τὰ μνημεῖα.
10. οἱ Φαρισαῖοι τοῦ συνεδρίου ποιοῦσιν ἱμάτιον τῷ Ἰησοῦ;

Exercise B:

1. γινώσκουσιν οἱ ἀδελφοὶ τὴν ἀγάπην τοῦ θεοῦ.
2. τὰ δαιμόνια φιλεῖ τὴν τοῦ θεοῦ διαθήκην;
3. εὐλογοῦμεν τὴν ὑπομονὴν τοῦ Χριστοῦ.
4. τὰ τέκνα λαμβάνει τὰ βιβλία τῆς γραφῆς;
5. ὁ Ἰησοῦς λαλεῖ τὰς παραβολὰς τῷ λαῷ τῆς κώμης.
6. πέμπεις τοὺς λόγους τοῦ εὐαγγελίου τῆς εἰρήνης.
7. ἐσθίομεν τὸν καρπὸν τῆς γῆς.
8. οἱ δοῦλοι μισοῦσιν τὴν φυλακήν.
9. οἱ ἀπόστολοι ἔχουσιν τὴν τιμὴν τῶν ἀνθρώπων.
10. ὁ Ἰάκωβος πέμπει ἐπιστολὴν τῷ φίλῳ τοῦ ἀποστόλου.

Exercise C:

1. ὁ θεὸς μισεῖ τὴν ἀδικίαν καὶ τὴν ἁμαρτίαν.
2. ἡ μετάνοια θύρα τῆς σωτηρίας ἐστίν.
3. ἡ γενεὰ ἁμαρτωλῶν μετανοεῖ;
4. ζητοῦσιν τὸν καιρὸν τῆς ἐπαγγελίας.
5. θεωροῦμεν τὴν ἀρχὴν τῆς ἡμέρας.
6. Χριστὸς ἔχει τὴν ἐξουσίαν τοῦ θεοῦ.
7. Πέτρος εὐλογεῖ τὸν Κύριον τῆς γῆς καὶ τῆς θαλάσσης.
8. ὁ Ἰησοῦς θεραπεύει τὸν υἱὸν τῆς χήρας.
9. ἡ ὥρα τῆς δόξης τοῦ Χριστοῦ χαρά ἐστιν τοῖς ἀγγέλοις.
10. Παῦλος ζητεῖ καρδίαν τῆς εἰρήνης καὶ τῆς δικαιοσύνης.

Lesson 7

1. ὑποκριτά, τηρεῖς τὰς ἐντολὰς ἀλλ᾽ οὐ φιλεῖς τὸν θεόν.
2. ὁ Παῦλος μαρτυρεῖ τῇ ἀληθείᾳ τοῦ εὐαγγελίου καὶ τῇ σοφίᾳ τοῦ θεοῦ.
3. οἱ ἐργάται βάλλουσιν λίθους εἰς τὴν θάλασσαν;
4. λέγει οὖν ὁ Ἰησοῦς, Ὁ υἱὸς τοῦ ἀνθρώπου ἐστὶν ἐν ταῖς τῶν οὐρανῶν νεφέλων.
5. ἔστιν Ἰησοῦς· σώζει γὰρ τὸν λαὸν ἀφ᾽ ἁμαρτίας.
6. οἱ ἐργάται οὐχ εὑρίσκουσιν τὴν ὁδὸν εἰς τὸν σταυρόν, καὶ τὴν θυσίαν τοῦ Ἰησοῦ οὐ
   θεωροῦσιν.
7. Ἰωάννης ἄρα γινώσκει τὸν ἀδελφὸν Ἰούδα.
8. οἱ στρατιῶται βάλλουσιν Ἀνδρέαν τὸν ἀπόστολον εἰς φυλακήν.
9. ἐν τῇ ἡμέρᾳ τῆς δόξης βλέπομεν τὸν Χριστὸν πρόσωπον πρὸς πρόσωπον.
10. ὁ οὖν κριτὴς οὐ λαμβάνει τὸ ἀργύριον ἀπὸ τῶν πρεσβυτέρων τῆς ἐκκλησίας, οὐδὲ
    μισεῖ τοὺς ἀποστόλους.

Lesson 8

1. ἐν ταῖς ἐσχάταις ἡμέραις ὀλίγοι ἔχουσιν τὴν ἀγάπην.
2. οἱ κακοὶ προφῆται οὐ μαρτυροῦσιν τῇ ἀληθείᾳ.
3. ὁ ἀπόστολος ὁ ἀγαπητὸς πρῶτον γράφει καινὴν ἐπιστολὴν τῇ ἐκκλησίᾳ.
4. ὁ Ἀνδρέας πρῶτος μαθητὴς τοῦ Χριστοῦ ἐστίν.
5. μόνος Παῦλος μένει πιστός;
6. ὁ Ἰησοῦς θεραπεύει τοὺς τυφλοὺς καὶ τοὺς λεπρούς.
7. οἱ φίλοι ἔχουσιν ἱκανὸν ἀργύριον.
8. τὰ λοιπὰ παιδία αἰτεῖ ἄρτον ἀπὸ τῶν ἀδελφῶν τοῦ Ἰησοῦ.
9. ὁ θεὸς κρίνει ἕκαστον νεανίαν.
10. οἱ σοφοὶ οὐ γινώσκουσιν τὸν θεὸν τῇ σοφίᾳ, ἀλλ᾽ οἱ πτωχοὶ ζητοῦσιν τὴν βασιλείαν τοῦ θεοῦ.

Lesson 9

1. μακάριοί εἰσιν οἱ καθαροὶ ἐν τῇ καρδίᾳ.
2. ὁ παλαιὸς οἶνός ἐστιν ἀγαθός, ὁ δὲ νέος ἐστὶν κακός.
3. οἱ ἅγιοι βλέπουσιν τὴν δόξαν τῶν οὐρανῶν καὶ μαρτυροῦσιν ταῖς φωναῖς τῶν ἀγγέλων.
4. ὦ ὑποκριτά, εἰ ὁ δοῦλος νεκρῶν ἔργων.
5. ὁ υἱὸς τοῦ ἀνθρώπου ἔχει τρίτον πειρασμὸν ἐν τῇ ἐρήμῳ.
6. ἐστὲ ἐχθροὶ τοῦ σταυροῦ τοῦ Χριστοῦ.
7. ἡ προσευχὴ τοῦ Φαρισαίου οὐκ ἔστιν καθαρά.
8. οἱ πλούσιοι οὐκ εἰσὶν ἐλεύθεροι ἀπὸ τῆς ἐξουσίας τοῦ θεοῦ.
9. ὁ θεὸς ἐγείρει τὸν Ἰησοῦν ἐκ τῶν νεκρῶν.
10. οἱ ἐχθροὶ Χριστοῦ εἰσιν τέκνα τοῦ διαβόλου.

Lesson 10

1. ὁ Ἰησοῦς παρελάμβανεν μικρὰ παιδία, καὶ τὰ μικρὰ παιδία ἤκουεν τοῦ Ἰησοῦ.
2. αἱ παρθένοι ὑπῆγον ἐκ τοῦ οἴκου.
3. ὁ δὲ Χριστὸς φέρει σταυρὸν καὶ περισσεύει ἐν ἀγάπῃ.
4. ἐχαίρομεν ἐν Κυρίῳ, ἦγεν γὰρ τὴν ἐκκλησίαν εἰς τὴν ἀλήθειαν.
5. οἱ προφῆται ἐδίδασκον τὰ τέκνα ἐν τῇ ἐρήμῳ.
6. ὁ Ἰησοῦς ἤνοιγεν τοὺς ὀφθαλμοὺς τῶν τυφλῶν, καὶ ἐπεγίνωσκεν τοὺς ἰδίους φίλους.
7. προσεφέρομεν τὸ ἀργύριον τῷ τελώνῃ, ἀλλ᾽ ἐδίωκεν τοὺς πλουσίους καὶ τοὺς πτωχούς.
8. οἱ ἐχθροὶ τοῦ λαοῦ ἀπέθνησκον ἐν φυλακῇ, ὁ δὲ κριτὴς ἀπέλυεν ὀλίγους δούλους.
9. Ἰωάννης ὁ βαπτιστὴς οὐκ ἐποίει σημεῖα.
10. οὐκ ἐδίδασκεν τὰ τέκνα, οὐδὲ ἀπῆγεν τὴν ἰδίαν γενεὰν ἀπὸ τῶν ὁδῶν τῆς ἀδικίας.

Lesson 11

Exercise A:

1. ἐκεῖνα δὲ τὰ δένδρα ἔβαλλον εἰς τὴν θάλασσαν.
2. οὗτοι οἱ πρεσβύτεροι δοκοῦσιν τυφλοί.
3. αὗται ἔμενον ἐν τῷ πλοίῳ.
4. οὗτος οὖν ὁ δεύτερος ἀδελφὸς διηκόνει καὶ προσεκύνει τῷ θεῷ ἐν ἑτέρῳ ἱερῷ.
5. παρεκαλοῦμεν καὶ ἐφωνοῦμεν, ἀλλ' οὐκ ἠκολούθουν.
6. οἱ πτωχοὶ ἐγάμουν καὶ κατῴκουν ἐν τῇ γῇ.
7. ὅλη γὰρ ἡ συναγωγὴ ἐδόκει ὁμοία προβάτοις.
8. ἡ ἀγάπη καὶ ἡ ἀλήθειά εἰσιν ἐν τῇ αἰωνίῳ βασιλείᾳ τοῦ θεοῦ.
9. ἐν τῇ ὥρᾳ ἐκείνῃ ἐχαίρομεν.
10. ἐκεῖνος ὁ πονηρὸς διάκονος ἔδει τὸν ἴδιον υἱόν.

Exercise B:

1. αὕτη ἐστὶν ἡ ἀγάπη τοῦ θεοῦ.
2. αἱ λοιπαὶ τῆς κώμης συνῆγον τὰ πρόβατα αὐτῶν ἐν μέσῳ τοῦ ἀγροῦ.
3. οἱ αὐτοὶ μαθηταὶ ηὐχαρίστουν τῷ πλουσίῳ τελώνῃ.
4. ἐκεῖνοι ἦσαν ἕτεροι ἄρτοι καὶ ἄλλο ποτήριον.
5. ἧς ὑποκριτὴς καὶ ἤμεθα τυφλοί.
6. αὐτοὶ παρελαμβάνομεν αὐτοὺς εἰς τὸ ἕτερον πλοῖον.
7. ἄλλο παιδίον βάλλει ἑαυτὸ εἰς τὴν θάλασσαν.
8. οἱ αὐτοὶ Ἰουδαῖοι οὗτοι ἤκουον καὶ ἠκολούθουν τοῖς ἰδίοις προφήταις.
9. ἤμην ἀγαπητός, ἀλλ' ἐμισεῖτε ἀλλήλους.
10. ἐβλέπετε τοὺς υἱοὺς αὐτῆς ἐν τῇ ἐκκλησίᾳ.

Lesson 12

Exercise A:

1. ὁ διδάσκαλός ἐστιν ὑπὲρ τὸν μαθητήν.
2. πτωχοὶ ἦσαν ἐν τῷ Ἰσραὴλ ἐπὶ Ἡλείου τοῦ προφήτου.
3. οὐκ ἐστὲ ὑπὸ νόμον, ἀλλ' ὑπὸ τὴν ἀγάπην.
4. ἐν τρίτῃ ἡμέρᾳ ἐζήτουν σημεῖον παρ' αὐτοῦ ἐκ τοῦ οὐρανοῦ.
5. ὑπῆγον κατ' ἰδίαν εἰς τὰς ἰδίας οἰκίας.
6. ὁ θεός ἐστιν ὑπὲρ τοῦ λαοῦ αὐτοῦ, ἀλλ' οἱ ἐργάται Σατανᾶ εἰσιν κατὰ τῆς ἐκκλησίας.
7. δι' ἀνθρώπου ἐστὶν ὁ θάνατος, ἀλλ' ὁ Χριστὸς τηρεῖ τοὺς ἰδίους μαθητὰς ἕως τῆς παρουσίας αὐτοῦ.
8. ἡ τῆς σωτηρίας χαρὰ περισσεύει χωρὶς τοῦ νόμου.
9. πρὸ ἐκείνης τῆς ὥρας οὐκ ἐθεώρουν τὴν δόξαν αὐτοῦ οὐδὲ ἤχουον τὴν φωνὴν αὐτοῦ.
10. ἡ αὐτὴ χήρα περιεπάτει περὶ τὴν κώμην.

Exercise B:

1. οὗτοι οἱ λόγοι ἐλαλοῦντο ὑπὸ τῶν ἀποστόλων ἐνώπιον τῶν πρεσβυτέρων.
2. ἐπέμπεσθε μετὰ τῶν προφητῶν ἔμπροσθεν τοῦ ὄχλου.

3. τὸ μνημεῖον ᾠκοδομεῖτο ὑπὸ τὸ ἱερόν.
4. ἦγες τὸν λαὸν ὀπίσω τοῦ ἀγαπητοῦ προφήτου διὰ τῆς ἔρημον εἰς τὰ Ἱεροσόλυμα.
5. οἱ φίλοι ἔπεμπον ὀλίγους ἄρτους πρὸς ἀλλήλους, καὶ ὀλίγον οἶνον καὶ ἱκανὸν ἀργύριον πρὸς τοὺς ἀξίους ἀδελφοὺς τοὺς ἐν φυλακῇ.
6. μετ' ἐκείνας τὰς ἡμέρας οἱ λοιποὶ στρατιῶται ὑπῆγον ἔξω τῆς κώμης.
7. ὦ ὑποκριτά, οὐ λαλεῖς περὶ τῶν ἐντολῶν τοῦ Κυρίου.
8. μετ' οὖν ταῦτα ἐλαλοῦμεν τὸν λόγον τοῦ θεοῦ τοῖς μαθηταῖς.
9. ἐκλαίετε ὑπὲρ τῶν ἀπίστων καὶ τῶν ἀκαθάρτων.
10. αὐτοὶ οἱ νεανίαι ἐδιδάσκοντο ὑπὸ τῶν ἰδίων διδασκάλων.

Lesson 13

1. λάμβανε τὸ ποτήριον καὶ χαῖρε ἐν τούτῳ τῷ δευτέρῳ σημείῳ τῆς δικαιοσύνης, τῆς εἰρήνης καὶ τῆς ζωῆς.
2. λύου ἀπὸ τῆς ἁμαρτίας καθ' ἡμέραν.
3. ἡ ἀρχὴ τῆς ἐξουσίας ἐστὶν ἢ δοκεῖ ὁμοία νέῳ οἴνῳ.
4. οὐχὶ ἡ πρώτη ἦν ἐσχάτη;
5. ὁ διδάσκαλος ὅς ἐστιν ἄξιος τῆς τιμῆς πιστευέτω τῷ βιβλίῳ καὶ προσκυνείτω τῷ θεῷ.
6. μήτι ἐκάλει κακοὺς εἰς τὸν φόβον τοῦ θεοῦ;
7. ἀνοίγετε ἑκάστην θύραν, τοῦτο γάρ ἐστιν δυνατὸν παρὰ τῷ θεῷ.
8. τὴν δικαιοσύνην ἐνδύετε τὴν καρδίαν καὶ θυσίαι προσφερέσθωσαν ἐν μέσῳ τοῦ ναοῦ.
9. οἱ νεκροὶ μή εἰσιν μακάριοι;
10. αἱ παρθένοι αἳ ἤσθιον τὸν ἄρτον οὐκ ἔκρινον ἑαυτάς.

Lesson 14

1. ἐμοὶ μὲν ἐδόκει σοφόν, οἱ δὲ ἠκολούθουν ἑτέρᾳ ὁδῷ.
2. κρατεῖτε ἐμέ, λαὲ Ἰουδαίας, καὶ σῴζετε ἑαυτοὺς ἐκ ταύτης τῆς πονηρᾶς γενεᾶς.
3. διηκόνουν σοι καὶ ἔδουν ἑαυτοὺς τῇ αἰωνίῳ διαθήκῃ σου.
4. κἀγὼ προσφέρω θυσίας, ἃς παραλαμβάνει ὁ θεός.
5. κἀγώ εἰμι ἐν μέσῳ ὑμῶν ὡς διάκονος.
6. τοῦτο δέ ἐστιν τὸ σημεῖον τῆς σῆς παρουσίας.
7. οὐκ εἰμὶ ὥσπερ οἱ λοιποὶ τῶν ἀνθρώπων.
8. ὁ δὲ λέγει ἡμῖν, Προσφέρετε τοὺς πτωχοὺς πρός με.
9. σὺ περὶ σεαυτοῦ μαρτυρεῖς· ἡ μαρτυρία σού ἐστιν ἀκάθαρτος.
10. ὁ διδάσκαλος ὃς οὐκ ἔστιν μετ' ἐμοῦ κατ' ἐμοῦ ἐστιν.

Lesson 15

Exercise A:

1. μὴ ἔξεστιν αὐτοῖς λαμβάνειν τὸ ἀργύριον ἀπὸ τῶν τελωνῶν;
2. αἱ νεφέλαι ὑπάγουσιν καὶ αἱ ψυχαὶ τῶν ἀνθρώπων θέλουσιν εὐχαριστεῖν.
3. ἠθέλομεν οὖν θεραπεύειν τοὺς υἱοὺς αὐτῶν.
4. καὶ διὰ τὸ περισσεύειν τὴν ἀδικίαν ἡ ἀγάπη ἀποθνήσκει;

5. ἔδει τὸν Ἰησοῦν ἀπάγειν τοὺς μαθητὰς ἀπὸ τῆς Γαλιλαίας.
6. οἱ δὲ ὄχλοι ἔχαιρον ἐν τῷ αὐτοὺς ἀκούειν καὶ βλέπειν τὰ σημεῖα ἃ ἐποίει.
7. ὁ ἄνεμος ἦν ἰσχυρὸς ὥστε βάλλειν τὸ πλοῖον ἐπὶ τὰς πέτρας.
8. μήτι δυνάμεθα ποιεῖν τοῦτο;
9. ἐν δὲ τῷ συνάγεσθαι τοὺς πρεσβυτέρους ἐμένομεν ἐν τοῖς ἀγροῖς.
10. οὐ μισῶ τὸν ἐχθρόν μου ὥστε με δύνασθαι τὸν θεὸν φιλεῖν.

Exercise B:

1. ἀνοίξω τὰ βιβλία ἃ ἐστιν ἐν τῇ συναγωγῇ.
2. πέμψω πρὸς αὐτοὺς σοφοὺς καὶ προφήτας, ἀλλ' οὐκ ἀκούσουσιν αὐτῶν οἱ υἱοὶ Ἰσραήλ.
3. οἱ λεπροὶ ἕξουσιν τὰ πρόβατα ἃ σώζεται ἀπὸ τῶν ἀνέμων καὶ τῆς θαλάσσης.
4. πείσομεν ἄρα τοὺς ἰδίους ἀδελφοὺς ἐκβάλλειν τοὺς δεξιοὺς ὀφθαλμοὺς αὐτῶν;
5. καὶ καλέσουσιν τὸ τέκνον Ἰησοῦν, σώζει γὰρ τὸν λαὸν αὐτοῦ ἀπὸ τῶν ἁμαρτιῶν αὐτῶν.
6. ἐν δὲ τῷ τὸν ὄχλον ἀκούειν τὸν λόγον τὰ δαιμόνια ἦγεν θυσίας τοῦ προσφέρειν αὐτὰς τῷ Σατανᾷ.
7. ἠσθένει δὲ τὸ δένδρον διὰ τὸ μὴ ἔχειν γῆν.
8. οὐχί ἐστιν ὁ καιρὸς τοῦ πιστεύειν;
9. θεωρήσομεν τὸ πρόσωπον τοῦ Κυρίου ἐν τῷ ἱερῷ ὃ οἰκοδομεῖται ἐν τοῖς Ἱεροσολύμοις.
10. διὸ φωνεῖ ἡμῖν καθ' ἡμέραν πρὸς τὸ παρακαλεῖν ἡμᾶς.

Lesson 16

Exercise A:

1. καθαρίζετε τὰς ἰδίας καρδίας καὶ περιπατήσετε ἐνώπιόν μου ἐν ὁδοῖς τῆς χαρᾶς.
2. κηρύσσετε τὰς ἐπαγγελίας καὶ φυλάσσετε τὰς ἐντολὰς ἐν τῷ ὑμᾶς ἐτοιμάζειν τὴν ὁδὸν τῆς δόξης.
3. ὁ δὲ πτωχὸς κράζει ἐν μέσῳ τοῦ ἱεροῦ.
4. πράσσετε τὴν δικαιοσύνην ἀλλήλοις καὶ δοξάσετε τὸν μόνον θεόν.
5. καὶ ἀποκαλύψω τὴν ἁμαρτίαν τῶν ἀνθρώπων οἳ πράσσουσιν τὴν ἀδικίαν, καὶ κρύψουσιν τοὺς ὀφθαλμοὺς αὐτῶν ἀπ' ἐμοῦ.
6. ἀπήρχοντο γὰρ πρὸς τὴν ἔρημον ἐν ᾗ αὐτὸς ὁ Ἰωάννης ἐβάπτιζεν.
7. κἀκεῖνος δέχεται τοὺς ἁμαρτωλοὺς οἳ ἔρχονται πρὸς αὐτὸν καὶ ἐσθίει μετ' αὐτῶν.
8. δεῖ ὑμᾶς ἀποκρίνεσθαι ταύτῃ τῇ γενεᾷ.
9. αὐτὸς ὁ Χριστὸς ἄρξει τῆς ἐκκλησίας, καὶ ὁ λαὸς αὐτοῦ προσεύξεται καὶ εὐαγγελίσεται.
10. ὁ δὲ οὐκ ἤθελεν πορεύεσθαι ἐν ταῖς ὁδοῖς τῆς ἀληθείας.

Lesson 17

Exercise A:

1. οὐδὲ ἐδίωξαν τοὺς τελώνας οἳ ἀπῆγον τὰ πρόβατα.
2. ἔπεμψας γὰρ τὰς χήρας ἀγοράσαι τὰ ἱμάτια.
3. διήρχεσθε τὴν καλὴν γῆν ἑτοιμάσαι τὸν ἐλεύθερον λαόν.

4. ἐργάτα ἰσχυρέ, κρῦψον τοὺς λίθους οἳ περισσεύουσιν ἐν τῷ ἀγρῷ.
5. καθαρίσατε καὶ ἁγιάσατε τὰς καρδίας ὑμῶν.
6. βούλονται δὲ ἀδικῆσαι τὴν τιμὴν τῶν λοιπῶν;
7. ἡ γὰρ φωνὴ τοῦ Ἰωάννου ἔκραξεν ἐν τῇ ἐρήμῳ, Ἑτοιμάσατε τὴν ὁδὸν τῷ Κυρίῳ.
8. καὶ ἐτηρήσαμεν τὰς ἐντολὰς ἃς ἠκούσαμεν ἀπὸ τῶν πιστῶν στρατιωτῶν.
9. καλόν ἐστιν αὐτοὺς τὰ αὐτὰ ἀναγινώσκειν.
10. μετὰ ταῦτα τὴν ἐξουσίαν μου καὶ τὰς χρείας μου ἀποκαλύψω αὐτοῖς.

Exercise B:

1. ἀνέβημεν εἰς τὸ ἱερὸν ἐν ἐκείνῃ τῇ ὥρᾳ.
2. ὦ Κύριε, ἥμαρτον ἐνώπιόν σου.
3. οἱ δὲ προφῆται ἔφυγον εἰς τὴν ἔρημον.
4. οὗτός ἐστιν ὁ λίθος ὃς ἔπεσεν ἐκ τοῦ οὐρανοῦ.
5. εὗρον δὲ τὸ ἀργύριον καὶ αὐτὸ ἤγαγον αὐτοῖς ὥστε αὐτοὺς παραλαβεῖν τὸν μισθὸν αὐτῶν.
6. οἴσει δὲ τὸν σταυρὸν καὶ πίεται τὸ ποτήριον.
7. ἔμαθον γὰρ παθεῖν καὶ ὄψονται τὸ πρόσωπον αὐτοῦ.
8. εἴδομεν δὲ τὸν ἥλιον καὶ εἴπομεν λόγους τῆς χαρᾶς καὶ τῆς μετανοίας.
9. λημψόμεθα τὴν δυνατὴν σωτηρίαν αὐτοῦ καὶ γνωσόμεθα τὴν εἰρήνην αὐτοῦ.
10. καὶ ἐν τῷ ἀγαγεῖν αὐτοὺς τὸ παιδίον τοῦ προσενεγκεῖν αὐτὸ τῷ Κυρίῳ, ὁ λαὸς ηὐλόγησεν τὸν θεόν.

Lesson 18

1. ὑμεῖς οὐ πιστεύετε, ὅτι οὐκ ἐστὲ ἐκ τῶν προβάτων τῶν ἐμῶν.
2. οὗτοι κρινοῦσιν τὰς χήρας καὶ ἀποκτενοῦσιν τὰ τέκνα αὐτῶν;
3. ἔμεινα δὲ ἐν τῷ ἰδίῳ τόπῳ ἕως ἀνέγνω τὸ βιβλίον.
4. ὁ δὲ Ἰησοῦς εἶπεν τῷ παραλυτικῷ, Ἆρον αὐτὸ καὶ ὕπαγε εἰς τὸν οἶκον σου· ὅτε δὲ ἤκουσεν ταῦτα ἦρεν αὐτὸ καὶ ὑπῆγεν.
5. εἶπον οὖν ὑμῖν ὅτι ἀποθανεῖσθε ἐν ταῖς ἁμαρτίαις ὑμῶν.
6. καὶ ἐροῦσιν ὅτι Ἀπέθανεν ἐν τῇ πρώτῃ ἡμέρᾳ ἕως ἠργαζόμεθα.
7. ὑμεῖς λέγετε ὅτι βλασφημεῖς, ὅτι εἶπον, Υἱὸς τοῦ θεοῦ εἰμι.
8. δύνασθε πίειν τὸ ποτήριον ὃ δεῖ με πιεῖν;
9. ἀλλ᾽ οἱ Φαρισαῖοι ἔλεγον ὅτι ἐσθίει παρὰ ἁμαρτωλῷ.
10. παρηγγείλατε αὐτοῖς μὴ ἀδικῆσαι ὅλον τὸν λαόν.

Lesson 19

1. ὑμεῖς μὲν ἠρνήσασθε τὸν ἅγιον καὶ δίκαιον κατ᾽ ἰδίαν, ὁ δὲ ἠρνήσατο αὐτὸν ἔμπροσθεν ὅλου τοῦ λαοῦ.
2. αὐτὸν δεῖ τὸν οὐρανὸν δέξασθαι, ἀλλ᾽ ὀψόμεθα αὐτὸν ἐν τῇ ἡμέρᾳ τῆς δευτέρας παρουσίας αὐτοῦ.
3. Πέτρε, ἐλθὲ εἰς τὴν οἰκίαν τῆς ἀπίστου καὶ ἄσπασαι αὐτήν.
4. μὴ γίνεσθε ὅμοιοι τοῖς ὑποκριταῖς, ἀλλὰ γίνεσθε πιστοὶ ἀλλήλοις.
5. ὁ δὲ πρῶτος παρεγένετο καὶ εἶπεν, Κύριε, Βουλόμεθα μαθεῖν προσεύξασθαι.
6. οὐκ ἔξεστιν προφήτῃ ἀπολέσθαι ἔξω τῶν Ἱεροσολύμων.

7. κἀκεῖνος ἀπώλετο, ἀλλ᾽ οἱ υἱοὶ αὐτοῦ οὐκ ἀπώλοντο.
8. καὶ ἐγένετο ἐν τῷ σπείρειν ἄλλα ἔπεσεν παρὰ τὴν ὁδόν.
9. ἐν τῷ κόσμῳ ἦν, καὶ ὁ κόσμος δι᾽ αὐτοῦ ἐγένετο, καὶ ὁ κόσμος αὐτὸν οὐκ ἔγνω.
10. ἦρξω ἀπὸ τῶν ἐσχάτων ἕως τῶν πρώτων.

Lesson 20

1. καὶ ἐγείρεσθε ταῖς χερσὶν τῆς γυναικός.
2. φυλασσέσθωσαν οἱ παῖδες ὑπὸ τῶν Ἑλλήνων.
3. γύναι, μὴ εὗρες ἱκανὸν ἀργύριον τοῖς ἄρχουσιν;
4. ἀλλὰ καλαὶ θυγατέρες γενήσονται ὅμοιαι ταῖς μητράσιν αὐτῶν.
5. ἀπηγγείλαμεν δὲ ὅτι ἐστὶν σωτὴρ ταῖς γυναιξίν.
6. οὐ μενοῦσιν ἐν τῇ γῇ αὐτῶν εἰς τῶν αὐτῶν;
7. ἴδε, ὦ γύναι, οἱ τῶν οὐρανῶν ἀστέρες μαρτυροῦσιν τῷ Σωτῆρι.
8. μετὰ τὸ ἀποθανεῖν τὸν πατέρα αὐτοῦ κατῴκησεν ἐν τῇ γῇ ταύτῃ.
9. καὶ αὐτὴν ἀπέκτεινεν τοῖς ποσὶν τῆς εἰκόνος ἣ ἔπεσεν ἐν μέσῳ τοῦ ναοῦ.
10. ὁ σωτήρ ἐστιν ὑπὲρ τὸν διδάσκαλον, ὅτι ἀπέθανεν ὑπὲρ τῶν προβάτων.

Lesson 21

1. ἔξομεν ἄρα βάπτισμα μετανοίας διὰ τοῦ αἵματος αὐτοῦ;
2. ἰσχυρὰ δὲ ῥήματα κρίματος ἐξῆλθεν ἐκ τοῦ στόματός σου.
3. εἶπεν οὖν ὅτι οὐκ ἔστιν τὸ φῶς, ἀλλ᾽ ἔρχεται μαρτυρῆσαι περὶ τοῦ φωτός.
4. μετὰ ταῦτα ἥψατο τοῦ ὠτὸς τῇ χειρὶ αὐτοῦ.
5. καὶ διήλθομεν διὰ πυρὸς καὶ ὕδατος, τὸ γὰρ πνεῦμα τοῦ ἐλέους κατῴκει ἡμᾶς.
6. ἀνοίξει δὲ τὰ ὦτα τῶν πληθῶν ἃ οὐ δύναται ἀκούειν.
7. ἴδετε τὰς χεῖρας καὶ τοὺς πόδας μου.
8. μὴ δύνανται οἱ πόδες εἰπεῖν ταῖς χερσὶν ὅτι χρείαν ὑμῶν οὐκ ἔχομεν, ὅτι οὐκ ἐστὲ μέλη τοῦ σώματος;
9. ἔβαλεν δὲ τὸ σπέρμα εἰς σκεῦος ἐν τῇ ἡμέρᾳ τοῦ πάσχα.
10. καὶ ἔσται τέρατα ἐν τῷ σκότει τῆς νυκτός, αἷμα καὶ πῦρ καὶ φόβος.

Lesson 22

1. παραλήψονται δὲ μισθὸν ὅς ἐστιν κρείσσων τῆς ζωῆς.
2. Ἀβραάμ, ἡ δικαιοσύνη σου περισσεύει, ὅτι ἐστὶν πλείων τῆς δικαιοσύνης τοῦ γένους σου.
3. καί τινες τῶν Φαρισαίων εἶπαν ἐν ἑαυτοῖς, Τί βλασφημεῖ;
4. τί σοι δοκεῖ, Σίμων; σὺ τίνα με λέγεις εἶναι;
5. οἱ δὲ ἀληθεῖς πρεσβύτεροι ἐν ἐλέει παρακαλοῦσιν τὰ ἀσθενῆ παιδία αὐτῶν.
6. τί με πειράζεις, ὑποκριτά; τίνος ἐστὶν ἡ εἰκὼν αὕτη;
7. δύναταί τις εἰσελθεῖν εἰς τὴν οἰκίαν τοῦ ἰσχυροῦ;
8. ὁ δὲ ἀδελφός σου ἔχει κατὰ σου.
9. λαλοῦσίν τινες κατὰ σάρκα, ἀλλὰ τὸ Πνεῦμά ἐστιν κατὰ τῆς σαρκός.
10. οὗτοί εἰσιν οἱ ἄνθρωποι οἵτινες ἀκούουσιν τὰ ῥήματα τοῦ πλήθους.

Lesson 23

1. καὶ οἱ ἄνδρες περιεπάτουν ἐν ταῖς πόλεσιν σὺν ταῖς γυναιξὶν αὐτοῦ.
2. παρήγγειλεν οὖν ταῖς ἰδίαις θυγατράσιν ἑτοιμάσαι τὸν ἰχθὺν τῷ βασιλεῖ.
3. καὶ δεῖ τοὺς γραμματεῖς λαβεῖν τοὺς ἰχθύας ἐκ τοῦ ὕδατος τοῖς ἱερεῦσιν.
4. καὶ ἐθαύμαζον ὅτι μετὰ τοῦ ἀρχιερέως ἐλάλει.
5. οὗτοί εἰσιν οἱ ἄνθρωποι οἵτινες λέγουσιν ἀνάστασιν μὴ εἶναι.
6. καὶ ἔσται χείρων χρόνος κρίσεως καὶ θλίψεως.
7. αἱ δὲ τῶν ἀνθρώπων παραδόσεις οὐκ ἄξουσιν τὴν ἄφεσιν τῶν ἁμαρτιῶν.
8. καὶ διώξουσιν ὑμᾶς ἀπὸ πόλεως εἰς πόλιν.
9. ὁ γὰρ μαθητὴς οὐ φιλεῖ πατέρα καὶ μητέρα ὑπὲρ ἐμέ.
10. ἐγὼ γὰρ παρὰ ἀνθρώπου οὐ παρέλαβον αὐτό, ἀλλὰ δι᾿ ἀποκαλύψεως.

Lesson 24

1. οἱ τέσσαρες λῃσταὶ ἔφυγον εἰς τὰ ὄρη.
2. οἱ ἓξ ἱερεῖς ἦλθον νυκτὸς καὶ ἦραν τὰ σώματα τῶν τριῶν προφητῶν.
3. ἀνοίξεις δὲ τὰ στόματα ἡμῶν, Κύριε, καὶ πᾶσα γλῶσσα εὐλογήσει τὸ μέγα ὄνομά σου.
4. μὴ βαστάζετε μηδένα εἰς τὴν συναγωγὴν ἐν τῷ σαββάτῳ.
5. καὶ πάντες οἱ μαθηταὶ πλήρεις πίστεως ἦσαν καὶ τοῦ Ἁγίου Πνεύματος, καὶ ἐθεράπευσαν τοὺς ἀσθενεῖς καὶ ἐξέβαλον πολλὰ δαιμόνια.
6. μηδεὶς σκανδαλιζέτω ἕνα τῶν παίδων τούτων.
7. ἐν δὲ ἐκείνῃ τῇ ὥρᾳ συνάγονται πρὸς αὐτὸν πολλοὶ τῶν ἀρχιερέων οἳ λέγουσιν ὅτι οὐκ ἔσται ἀνάστασις.
8. ὁ δὲ ἑκατοντάρχης ἀπεκρίνατο, Ἐγώ εἰμι [or: Ἐγὼ εἰμὶ κτλ.] ἄνθρωπος ὑπὸ ἐξουσίαν καὶ ἔχω ἑκατὸν στρατιώτας ὑπ᾿ ἐμέ.
9. ὅτε ἦλθον εἰς τὰς ἓξ κώμας ἐκήρυξαν τὸ εὐαγγέλιον πᾶσιν τοῖς ἔθνεσιν ἃ κατῴκει ἐν αὐταῖς.
10. ὁ χιλίαρχος καὶ χίλιοι ἄνδρες περιεπάτουν ἐν ταῖς τρισὶν πόλεσιν.

Lesson 25

1. γῆ Σοδόμων ἀνεκτότερον ἔσται ἐν ἡμέρᾳ κρίσεως ἢ σοί (or ἤ σοι).
2. οὐαί, οὐχὶ ἡ ψυχὴ πλεῖόν ἐστιν τῆς τροφῆς;
3. Ἰδοὺ ἡ ἐλπὶς καὶ ἡ ἀγάπη μείζονές εἰσιν τῆς πίστεως, μάλιστα ἡ ἀγάπη.
4. ὁ νεώτερος τῶν υἱῶν οὐκ ἤθελεν ἐργάζεσθαι ὑπὲρ τοῦ πατρὸς αὐτοῦ.
5. αἴρει γὰρ τὸ πλήρωμα αὐτοῦ ἀπὸ τοῦ ἱματίου καὶ χεῖρον σχίσμα γίνεται.
6. ἀμὴν λέγω ὑμῖν Ὅτε ἐποιήσατε ἑνὶ τούτων τῶν ἀδελφῶν μου τῶν ἐλαχίστων, ἐμοὶ ἐποιήσατε.
7. ναί, ἀπεκτείνατε τὸν σοφώτατον τῶν ἀνθρώπων.
8. ὁ δὲ ἔκραξεν μᾶλλον, Ἰδοὺ πάσχω ταῖς χερσὶν τῶν ἐχθρῶν μου.
9. λέγω ὑμῖν Μείζων ἐν γεννητοῖς γυναικῶν Ἰωάννου οὐδείς ἐστιν· ὁ δὲ μικρότερος ἐν τῇ βασιλείᾳ τοῦ θεοῦ μείζων αὐτοῦ ἐστιν.
10. δεῖ ἡμᾶς ὑπακούειν τῷ βασιλεῖ ἢ τῷ ἱερεῖ.

Lesson 26

1. παιδία, ἐσκάτη ὥρα ἐστίν, καὶ καθὼς ἠκούσατε ὅτι ἀντίχριστος ἔρχεται, καὶ νῦν ἀντίχριστοι πολλοὶ γεγόνασιν.
2. οὐ γέγραπται Ὁ οἶκός μου οἶκος προσευχῆς;
3. ὁ δὲ ἀπεκρίνατο, Ὃ γέγραφα, γέγραφα.
4. Χριστὸς ἀπέθανεν καὶ ἐγήγερται τῇ ἡμέρᾳ τῇ τρίτῃ.
5. οἱ δὲ τέσσαρες γραμματεῖς εὑρήκασιν πάντα τὰ μεγάλα σκεύη.
6. καὶ ἦσαν ἄνθρωποι οἵτινες φόνον πεποιήκεισαν.
7. θέλω δὲ ὑμᾶς εἰδέναι ὅτι παντὸς ἀνδρὸς ἡ κεφαλὴ ὁ Χριστός ἐστιν.
8. οὐδεὶς ἐδύνατο αὐτὸν δῆσαι, διὰ τὸ αὐτὸν πολλάκις δεδέσθαι.
9. πτωχὸς δέ τις ὀνόματι Λάζαρος ἐβέβλητο πρὸς τὸν πυλῶνα αὐτοῦ.
10. ὁ δὲ θεὸς λελάληκεν ταῦτα τὰ ῥήματα εἰς τὸ εἰδέναι ὑμᾶς τίς ἐστιν ἡ ἐλπὶς τῆς κλήσεως αὐτοῦ.

Lesson 27

1. πολλὰ τῶν ῥημάτων τούτων ἐγράφη ἐν βιβλίῳ ὑπὸ τοῦ ἀρχιερέως.
2. ἤχθη δὲ ὁ Ἰησοῦς ὑπὸ τοῦ πνεύματος εἰς τὰ ὄρη πειρασθῆναι ὑπὸ τοῦ διαβόλου.
3. οἱ νεκροὶ ἐγερθήσονται ἐν τῇ ἡμέρᾳ τῆς κρίσεως τῇ φωνῇ τοῦ ἀγγέλου.
4. οἴδαμεν ὅτι τοῦτο τὸ εὐαγγέλιον κηρυχθήσεται πᾶσιν τοῖς ἔθνεσιν καὶ πολλοὶ ἀκούσονται.
5. ἐν ἐκείνῃ τῇ ἡμέρᾳ πολλὰ σώματα τῶν ἁγίων ἠγέρθη, καὶ ἦλθεν εἰς τὴν πόλιν, καὶ ὤφθη πολλοῖς.
6. πάντες οἱ ἰχθύες ἐβλήθησαν εἰς τὸ ὕδωρ.
7. διδάσκαλε, φιληθήσῃ ὑπὸ παντὸς τοῦ ἔθνους.
8. οἱ δὲ νεανίαι ἐστράφησαν ἀπὸ τῶν ἁμαρτιῶν αὐτῶν ὅτι φόβος μέγας εἰλήφει αὐτούς.
9. καὶ πεπώκαμεν τὸ ποτήριον τῆς χαρᾶς ὃ ἀπέσταλκεν ὁ θεός.
10. διὰ τὸ ὄνομά μου ἀχθήσεσθε εἰς βασιλεῖς καὶ ἄρχοντας.

Lesson 28

Exercise A:

1. καὶ παράγων παρὰ τήν θάλασσαν τῆς Γαλιλαίας εἶδεν Σίμωνα.
2. καὶ ἦσαν οἱ φαγόντες τοὺς ἄρτους πεντακισχίλιοι ἄνδρες.
3. πολλοὶ οὖν τῶν τελωνῶν ἐβαπτίσθησαν μετανοοῦντες ἀπὸ τῶν ἁμαρτιῶν αὐτῶν.
4. ἀκούων δὲ Ἀνανίας τοὺς λόγους τούτους πεσὼν ἀπέθανεν, καὶ ἐγένετο φόβος μέγας ἐπὶ πάντας τοὺς ἀκούοντας.
5. ἐφοβούμεθα δὲ μὴ πιστεύοντες ὅτι τὸ ἔλεος αὐτοῦ ἀληθές ἐστιν.
6. οὗτος γάρ ἐστιν ὁ πεμφθεὶς ὑπὸ τοῦ βασιλέως.
7. καὶ ὤφθη αὐτοῖς Μωϋσῆς καὶ Ἠλείας συλλαλοῦντες μετ᾽ αὐτοῦ.
8. καὶ μὴ φοβεῖσθε ἀπὸ τῶν ἀποκτεινόντων τὸ σῶμα, τὴν δὲ ψυχὴν μὴ δυναμένων ἀποκτεῖναι· φοβεῖσθε μᾶλλον τὸν δυνάμενον καὶ ψυχὴν καὶ σῶμα ἀπολέσαι ἐν γεέννῃ.
9. πορευθέντες δὲ ἀπήγγειλεν τοῖς ἀρχιερεῦσιν ἅπαντα τὰ γενόμενα.
10. ταύτην δὲ θυγατέρα Ἀβραὰμ οὖσαν, ἣν ἔδησεν ὁ Σατανᾶς δέκα καὶ ὄκτω ἔτη, οὐκ ἔδει λυθῆναι τῇ ἡμέρᾳ τοῦ σαββάτου;

Exercise B:

1. ἐγγὺς δὲ οὔσης Λύδδας τῇ Ἰόππῃ, οἱ μαθηταὶ ἀκούσαντες ὅτι Πέτρος ἐστὶν ἐκεῖ, ἀπέστειλαν δύο ἄνδρας πρὸς αὐτόν.
2. ἀλλὰ λήμψεσθε δύναμιν σήμερον, ἐλθόντος τοῦ ἁγίου πνεύματος ἐφ᾽ ὑμᾶς.
3. τῆς ἡμέρας ἐγγισάσης ὁ υἱὸς τοῦ ἀνθρώπου ἐλεύσεται μετὰ τῶν νεφελῶν τοῦ οὐρανοῦ.
4. κρατοῦντος δὲ αὐτοῦ τὴν χεῖρά μου ἐδεξάμην δύναμιν περιπατεῖν.
5. καὶ ἦν ὁ Ἰωάννης ἐνδεδυμένος τρίχας καμήλου.
6. ἐγγιζόντων δὲ αὐτῶν τῇ πόλει ὅλον τὸ πλῆθος ἔχαιρεν λέγον, Μακάριος ὁ ἐρχόμενος ἐν ὀνόματι τοῦ Κυρίου.
7. ὧδε ἐν Ἱεροσολύμοις ἐστὶν ὁ τόπος ὅπου προσκυνεῖν δεῖ.
8. ὕπαγε εἰς τὸν οἶκόν σου πρὸς τοὺς σούς, καὶ ἀπάγγειλον αὐτοῖς ὅσα ὁ Κύριός σοι πεποίηκεν.
9. πῶς εἰσῆλθες ὧδε μὴ ἔχων ἔνδυμα γάμου;
10. καὶ τοιαύταις παραβολαῖς πολλαῖς ἐλάλει αὐτοῖς τὸν λόγον.

Lesson 29

1. ἐμὸν βρῶμά ἐστιν ἵνα ποιῶ τὸ θέλημα τοῦ πέμψαντός με.
2. ἀμὴν λέγω ὑμῖν ὅτι οὐ μὴ παρέλθῃ ἡ γενεὰ αὕτη ἕως ἂν πάντα ταῦτα γένηται.
3. ἄγωμεν εἰς τὰς ἄλλας κώμας, ἵνα καὶ ἐκεῖ κηρύξω.
4. ὃς ἂν ἓν τῶν τοιούτων παιδίων δέξηται ἐπὶ τῷ ὀνόματί μου, ἐμὲ δέχεται· καὶ ὃς ἂν ἐμὲ δέχηται, οὐκ ἐμὲ δέχεται, ἀλλὰ τὸν ἀποστείλαντά με.
5. ὃ ἐὰν δήσῃς ἐπὶ τῆς γῆς ἔσται δεδεμένον ἐν τοῖς οὐρανοῖς.
6. τί ποιήσωμεν; μένωμεν ἐν ἁμαρτίᾳ ἵνα περισσεύῃ ἡ χάρις;
7. πάντοτε γὰρ τοὺς πτωχοὺς ἔχετε, καὶ ὅταν θέλητε δύνασθε αὐτοῖς εὖ ποιῆσαι.
8. ὅπου ἐὰν κηρυχθῇ τὸ εὐαγγέλιον τοῦτο ἐν ὅλῳ τῷ κόσμῳ, λαληθήσεται καὶ ὃ ἐποίησεν αὕτη.
9. καὶ παρεκάλει αὐτοὺς ἵνα μετ᾽ αὐτοῦ ὦσιν, καὶ ἔλεγον ὅτι Προσεύχεσθε ἵνα μὴ ἔλθητε εἰς πειρασμόν.
10. καί τινες τῶν ὧδε ὄντων οὐ μὴ γεύσωνται θανάτου ἕως ἂν ἴδωσιν τὸν υἱὸν τοῦ ἀνθρώπου.

Lesson 30

1. τί οὖν ἐροῦμεν; ἐπιμένωμεν τῇ ἁμαρτίᾳ, ἵνα ἡ χάρις πλεονάσῃ; μὴ γένοιτο.
2. τὸ ἀργύριόν σου σὺν σοὶ εἴη εἰς ἀπώλειαν.
3. ἐάν τις θέλῃ τὸ θέλημα αὐτοῦ ποιεῖν, γνώσεται περὶ τῆς διδαχῆς.
4. εἰ ἠπίστησάν τινες, μὴ ἡ ἀπιστία αὐτῶν τὴν πίστιν τοῦ θεοῦ καταργήσει; μὴ γένοιτο· γινέσθω δὲ ὁ θεὸς ἀληθής, πᾶς δὲ ἄνθρωπος ψεύστης.
5. πάντα γὰρ ὑμῶν ἐστιν, εἴτε Παῦλος εἴτε Ἀπολλὼς εἴτε Κηφᾶς, εἴτε κόσμος εἴτε ζωὴ εἴτε θάνατος, πάντα ὑμῶν, ὑμεῖς δὲ Χριστοῦ, Χριστὸς δὲ θεοῦ.
6. ἐν τῇ πρώτῃ μου ἀπολογίᾳ οὐδείς μοι παρεγένετο, ἀλλὰ πάντες με ἐγκατέλιπον· μὴ αὐτοῖς λογισθείη.
7. γέγραπται γὰρ ἐν βίβλῳ ψαλμῶν ὅτι Τὴν ἐπισκοπὴν αὐτοῦ λάβοι ἕτερος.
8. ὁ γραμματεὺς ἔμεινεν ἐν τῷ ὄρει τεσσαράκοντα ἡμέρας καὶ τεσσαράκοντα νύκτας γράφων πάσας τὰς ἐντολὰς τοῦ νόμου.

9. ἐὰν ᾔδει ὁ οἰκοδεσπότης ποίᾳ φυλακῇ ὁ κλέπτης ἔρχεται, ἐγρηγόρησεν ἄν.
10. καὶ πάντες διελογίζοντο ἐν ταῖς καρδίαις αὐτῶν περὶ τοῦ Ἰωάννου μήποτε αὐτὸς εἴη ὁ Χριστός.

Lesson 31

1. καὶ ἠρώτησεν παρ' αὐτῶν ποῦ ὁ Χριστὸς γεννᾶται.
2. οἱ μαθηταὶ ἐφανέρουν ταῦτα ἃ ἤκουσαν.
3. ὁ δὲ θεὸς δικαιοῖ τοὺς υἱοὺς τῶν ἀνθρώπων πίστει καὶ οὐκ ἔργοις.
4. ὁ καυχώμενος ἐν Κυρίῳ καυχάσθω.
5. καὶ ἦλθον πρὸς τὸν ἱερέα ἵνα ἐρωτήσωσιν αὐτὸν περὶ τῆς συνειδήσεως αὐτῶν.
6. ἔλεγον τὴν ἔξοδον αὐτοῦ ἣν ἤμελλεν πληροῦν ἐν Ἰερουσαλήμ.
7. ἀκούσας δὲ ὄχλου διαπορευομένου ἐπηρώτησεν τί ἂν εἴη τοῦτο.
8. πλανᾶσθε μὴ εἰδότες τὰς γραφὰς μηδὲ τὴν δύναμιν τοῦ θεοῦ.
9. ὦ Πάτερ, φανέρωσον τὴν δύναμίν σου ἡμῖν ἵνα δοξασθῇ τὸ ὄνομά σου.
10. ἐθεώρουν τὸ ἱερὸν πεπληρωμένον τῇ δόξῃ τοῦ Κυρίου.

Lesson 32

1. καὶ λαβὼν τὸ σῶμα ὁ Ἰωσὴφ ἔθηκεν αὐτὸ ἐν τῷ καινῷ μνημείῳ αὐτοῦ.
2. καὶ αὐτὸς θεὶς τὰ γόνατα προσηύχετο.
3. καταβήσομαι ἵνα θῶ τὰς χεῖρας ἐπ' αὐτὴν καὶ ζήσει.
4. δεῖ ἡμᾶς τιθέναι τὸν νόμον τῆς ἀγάπης ἐν ταῖς καρδίαις ἡμῶν καθ' ἡμέραν.
5. πῶς θῶμεν τὴν θυγατέρα ἡμῶν παρὰ τοὺς πόδας αὐτοῦ;
6. τί ὅτι ἔθου ἐν τῇ καρδίᾳ σου τὸ πρᾶγμα τοῦτο;
7. καὶ ἐζήτουν αὐτὸν εἰσενεγκεῖν καὶ θεῖναι αὐτὸν ἐνώπιον αὐτοῦ.
8. οὐχ ὑμῶν ἐστιν γνῶναι χρόνους ἢ καιροὺς οὓς ὁ πατὴρ ἔθετο ἐν τῇ ἰδίᾳ ἐξουσίᾳ.
9. ὁ ποιμὴν ὁ καλὸς τὴν ψυχὴν αὐτοῦ τίθησιν ὑπὲρ τῶν προβάτων.
10. οἱ ἀπόστολοι κατηυλόγησαν ἡμᾶς ἐπιτιθέντες τὰς χεῖρας ἐφ' ἡμᾶς.

Lesson 33

1. εἰπέ μοι εἰ τὸ χωρίον ἀπέδοσθε· ἀπόδος μοι, εἴ τί ὀφειλεῖς.
2. ταῦτα πάντα σοι δώσω ἐὰν πεσὼν προσκυνήσῃς μοι.
3. ὁ δὲ οὐκ ἤθελεν, ἀλλὰ ἀπελθὼν ἔβαλεν αὐτὸν εἰς φυλακὴν ἕως ἀποδῷ τὸ ὀφειλόμενον.
4. τηρήσωμεν τὰς ἐντολὰς τὰς ἡμῖν διδομένας.
5. ὁ βασιλεὺς ἡμῖν δέδωκεν ταύτην τὴν πόλιν· μὴ παραδῶμεν αὐτὴν τοῖς ἐχθροῖς αὐτοῦ.
6. ἐδόθη μοι πᾶσα ἐξουσία ἐν οὐρανῷ καὶ ἐπὶ γῆς.
7. ὁ διδοὺς ἄρτον τοῖς ἀσθενέσιν ἕξει τὸν μισθὸν αὐτοῦ.
8. περιεπάτουν δὲ διδόντες ἱμάτια τοῖς λεπροῖς.
9. δεδώκεισαν δὲ οἱ ἀρχιερεῖς ἐντολάς.
10. καὶ ὅταν ἄγωσιν ὑμᾶς παραδιδόντες, μὴ προμεριμνᾶτε τί λαλήσητε, ἀλλ' ὃ ἐὰν δοθῇ ἐν ἐκείνῃ τῇ ὥρᾳ, τοῦτο λαλεῖτε.

Lesson 34

1. ταῦτα δὲ αὐτῶν λαλούντων αὐτὸς ἔστη ἐν μέσῳ αὐτῶν.
2. τὰ νῦν παραγγέλλει ὁ θεὸς τοῖς ἀνθρώποις πάντας πανταχοῦ μετανοεῖν, καθ᾽ ὅτι ἔστησεν ἡμέραν ἐν ᾗ μέλλει κρίνειν τὴν οἰκουμένην ἐν δικαιοσύνῃ.
3. ὁ δὲ Ἰησοῦς ἐστάθη ἔμπροσθεν τοῦ ἡγεμόνος.
4. δεῖ οὖν τὸν Παῦλον στῆναι ἐν τῷ συνεδρίῳ.
5. ἔβλεψαν σὺν αὐτοῖς ἑστῶτα τὸν ἄνθρωπον τὸν τεθεραπευμένον.
6. ἄνθρωπε, τίς με κατέστησεν κριτὴν ἐφ᾽ ὑμᾶς;
7. ἡ μήτηρ καὶ οἱ ἀδελφοὶ αὐτοῦ εἱστήκεισαν ἔξω ζητοῦντες αὐτῷ λαλῆσαι.
8. δοὺς δὲ αὐτῇ τὴν χεῖρα ἀνέστησεν αὐτήν.
9. πορεύεσθε καὶ σταθέντες λαλεῖτε ἐν τῷ ἱερῷ πάντα τὰ ῥήματα τῆς ζωῆς ταύτης.
10. εἴ τις πιστεύει εἰς ἐμὲ ἀναστήσω αὐτὸν ἐν τῇ ἐσχάτῃ ἡμέρᾳ.

Lesson 35

1. ὁ δέ φησιν Πᾶσα ἁμαρτία καὶ βλασφημία ἀφεθήσεται τοῖς ἀνθρώποις.
2. οὐκ εἴπομεν καθώς φασίν τινές ἡμᾶς λέγειν.
3. καὶ ἄφες ἡμῖν τὰ ὀφειλήματα ἡμῶν, ὡς καὶ ἡμεῖς ἀφήκαμεν τοῖς ὀφειλέταις ἡμῶν.
4. ὁ δὲ ἔφη Κύριε, σῶσον, ἀπολλύμεθα.
5. ὁ δέ φησίν Ἀφέωνται αἱ ἁμαρτίαι αὐτῆς αἱ πολλαί.
6. ἐν δὲ παραβολαῖς τὰ πάντα γίνεται μήποτε ἐπιστρέψωσιν καὶ ἀφεθῇ αὐτοῖς.
7. τότε δείκνυσιν αὐτῷ ὁ διάβολος πάσας τὰς βασιλείας τοῦ κόσμου.
8. καὶ ὅπου ἂν εἰσεπορεύετο ἐν ταῖς ἀγοραῖς ἐτίθεσαν τοὺς ἀσθενοῦντας.
9. ἐκείνοις δὲ τοῖς ἔξω ἐν παραβολαῖς τὰ πάντα γίνεται, ἵνα ἀκούοντες ἀκούσωσιν καὶ μὴ συνιῶσιν.
10. πάντες γὰρ οἱ λαβόντες μάχαιραν ἐν μαχαίρῃ ἀπολοῦνται.